The Securities Brokerage Industry

The Securities Brokerage Industry

Nonprice Competition and Noncompetitive Pricing

Lawrence Shepard
University of California, Davis

Lexington Books
D.C. Heath and Company
Lexington, Massachusetts
Toronto London

Library of Congress Cataloging in Publication Data

Shepard, Lawrence.
The securities brokerage industry.

Bibliography: p.
1. Brokers–United States. 2. Competition. 3. United States. Securities and Exchange Commission. I. Title.
HG4910.S43 332.6'42'0973 74-33804
ISBN 0-669-99135-x

Published simultaneously in Canada.

Printed in the United States of America.

International Standard Book Number: 0-669-99135-x

Library of Congress Catalog Card Number: 74-33804

To Nancy

Contents

List of Figures

List of Tables

Preface

To the skeptical eye of the industrial organization economist, three features distinguish the American brokerage industry: an extensive degree of nonprice competition, strikingly noncompetitive pricing and entry policies, and a seemingly unconcerned regulatory authority. The first phenomenon, nonprice competition, has taken the form of a vast array of auxilliary services that brokerage firms offer to attract customers. A single visit to a brokerage office or a perusal of the financial press bears evidence that a high degree of rivalry exists between firms in the services they provide to customers without charge. Industry participants have, however, carefully avoided price competition by collusively establishing commission rates. The Constitution of the New York Stock Exchange prescribes both minimum commission rates to be charged by firms on Exchange business and severe penalties for those who would charge less. That covenant also serves to restrict market entry by limiting the number of Exchange members. This further insulates the brokerage houses from the competitive forces encountered elsewhere. The overseer of both the brokerage industry and the securities markets, the Securities and Exchange Commission, represents a classic case of the regulators championing the regulated. In an important sense, the Commission's administration of industry "self regulation" has become an umbrella under which noncompetitive pricing and entry practices have flourished. Under federal regulation, NYSE brokerage has been characterized by antitrust immunity, exclusive franchise, barriers to entry, and uniform pricing.

The study described in the following pages has as its central purpose an analysis of these competitive features of the brokerage industry. In particular, it discusses forms of customer service competition as well as its dimensions. The effectiveness of price collusion within the industry and the height of barriers to entry are assessed. Reasons for and effects of SEC permissiveness are also analyzed. With this background, the book poses the broad question: to what extent has competition through customer services offset the profit associated with the noncompetitive pricing and entry policies of brokerage firms? It is believed that this represents the first comprehensive study in an industrial organization context of the market for securities brokerage.

The study follows the structure-conduct-performance paradigm familiar to students of industrial organization. Under the heading of "Market Structure," the first two chapters introduce the operations and organization of the brokerage industry. From this basis, successive chapters develop characteristics of industry pricing policy, regulation, and nonprice competition pertinent to the research topic. Finally, the impact of these forces on industry performance is analyzed in two lengthy chapters. After reviewing received theories of nonprice competition, the first considers the theoretical significance of patterns of industry behavior. The second employs an econometric model to estimate the relative effects of noncompetitive pricing and customer service competition on broker profits. Chapter 8 summarizes the findings and applies them to policy issues. New York Stock Exchange commission rate schedules for the period 1900-1974 are collectively reported, apparently for the first time, in the Appendix. The analysis is based on developments within the industry through May 15, 1974.

Acknowledgments

I wish to thank the National Science Foundation for personal support during the completion of this project in 1974. Certain research expenses were met by the Patent Fund of the Regents of the University of California. The Department of Economics of the University of California, Santa Barbara provided computer funds as well.

Several people have been helpful in guiding and expediting my work. My brother, mentor, and friend, Professor W. Bruce Shepard, encouraged me to take on this project by his enthusiastic reception of an earlier piece of research. Dr. Richard B. Heflebower helped shape this study in its earliest stage. Professor Llad Phillips read and criticized two drafts of the book. Dr. Mortimer Andron's contributions have been twofold: first, his friendship and tutelage have furthered my interest in the securities markets since my undergraduate days; in addition, his familiarity with the financial sector provided an important perspective in criticizing this project. I am especially indebted to Professor Walter Mead who proposed the topic as a subject of my dissertation research. His frequently expressed commitment to the use of economic analysis to solve real problems has left its mark on this research and this researcher.

Anyone who has written a book will attest that many burdens fall on family and friends. Beyond keeping the home fires burning, my wife provided sustenance and crucial encouragement at every turn. During the past months she so often helped me rekindle when the flame threatened to go out.

Part I: Market Structure

1 The Brokerage Industry

The markets for stocks and bonds perform many essential and useful functions in the United States economy. One of the most important is the influence which this market, along with other financial and non-financial institutions, exerts in allocating the nation's capital among numerous competing uses for these resources. The efficiency with which th[is] allocative function is performed determines in large part the overall growth and efficiency of the economy itself.

– William Baumol

Firms in the securities brokerage industry buy and sell stocks and bonds for their customers. In the representative transaction, brokerage houses do not own the securities changing hands. Thus, rather than selling securities, the firms sell a service, securities brokerage. In consideration for this service, brokers charge both buyers and sellers a commission based upon the value of the securities involved in each transaction. Most firms are equipped to execute their customers' orders within fifteen minutes. The industry thereby serves short term traders as well as those individuals and institutions who accumulate securities for investment purposes. Through its network of branch offices in cities of all sizes, the brokerage industry represents the primary link between the public and the equity markets of the United States.

Brokerage Operations

Securities brokerage is comprised of the sales, communications, execution, cashiering, and clearing functions. The sales function lies mainly in the domain of individual stock brokers or "registered representatives." Other functions are performed solely by nonbroker staff members. However, nonbroker personnel also assist registered representatives in providing certain free customer services associated

William Baumol, *The Stock Market and Economic Efficiency*, p. vii.

with the sales function. These free services will be discussed in detail in Chapter 5.

Registered representatives are primarily responsible for selling brokerage services. To prepare them for this role, brokerage houses sponsor broker training programs. The typical program includes six months of instruction in New York as well as later on-the-job supervision. Merrill, Lynch, Pierce, Fenner, and Smith estimates the cost of training a registered representative at $15,000.[1] According to the Securities and Exchange Commission (SEC), this instruction is largely sales-related. As a result, some brokers have been found to be ignorant of investment principles and back office procedures.[2] Upon completion of the New York Stock Exchange registration exams, brokers become salaried employees of the sponsoring brokerage house. Within one year they are expected to support themselves from their twenty to forty-five percent share of the commissions they generate.[3] Both the training and the basis of remuneration of registered representatives underscore their sales orientation.

In addition to placing orders, registered representatives extend many customer services related to their role as buying and selling agents. For example, brokers provide clients with investment information and frequently advise them about their holdings. Registered representatives follow the market performance of customers' stocks and bonds, keeping abreast of news events that might influence securities prices. In providing these services, stock brokers work closely with their customers. They are sometimes the customer's only link with the brokerage firm. Frequently the client's allegiance to his broker is stronger than is his affiliation with the firm.[4]

In making brokerage sales, registered representatives operate in well appointed offices or "board rooms." These facilities are designed to assist in the sales function in several ways. For example, board room libraries offer customers investment information on potential security purchases. Brokerage offices contain electronic devices that inform both clients and brokers of stock price changes. Also, the central location and comfortable furnishings of these facilities serve to attract customers.

For every salesman in the board room, the industry employs two "back office" employees to process transactions.[5] After an order is placed by a registered representative, nonbroker personnel transmit it to the point of execution via private wire. In the case of a transaction involving a security traded on an exchange, the order is channeled to the firm's representative on the floor of the exchange. That representative, an officer of the firm and a member of the exchange, moves to the area on the exchange floor where the security is traded. There he executes the transaction with a representative of another firm who has a complementary order. In the absence of a complementary order he deals with the exchange specialist who maintains an inventory of the security and a list of unfilled orders. Within minutes of execution, details of the transaction are wired to the originating broker. Confirmation of the order is mailed to the customer.

The associated cashiering and security clearing functions are also performed by back office help. For the brokerage firm, each transaction involves two parties: the firm's customer and the brokerage house with which the order is executed on the floor of the exchange. When a client makes a sale, he tenders the security certificate to his registered representative. The client's account is credited with the amount of the sale less the commission. At the same time, the certificate is delivered for payment to the brokerage house whose customer purchased the securities.[6] The back office staff of the purchasing firm debits their customer's account by the amount of the transaction plus the commission. They subsequently arrange with a stock transfer agent to have certificates issued in the new owner's name. A major brokerage house estimates that these labor intensive back office procedures require forty different steps.[7]

Like registered representatives and board room facilities, back office staff members contribute to sales by performing customer services related to the sales function. Among the many public services these employees perform are the preparation, reproduction, and distribution of market advisories, which customers use in making investment decisions. Back office employees hold in safekeeping stocks and bonds belonging to customers. They also arrange redemption of securities owned by clients in connection with tender offers and mergers. As a rule, such services are provided without charge for the benefit of customers.

In contrast with stock brokers, the employees who are in charge of back office operations receive very little formal training. According to the president of the largest brokerage house, few firms have in the past "bothered with the development of proper practices of recruitment and training" of back office help.[8] Even security analysts, perhaps the most specialized of nonbroker employees, have been found to lack adequate preparation. In spite of the fact that securities analysis involves application of statistics, economics, and finance, over forty percent of the analysts surveyed by the SEC had received no formal education beyond high school. A majority of them did not possess prior experience in the industry.[9] The lack of training and experience among nonbroker employees has been widely recognized as a source of the industry's inability to adjust smoothly to changes in brokerage volume.[10]

As has been discussed, registered representatives, back office employees, and brokerage offices are important in the provision of stock brokerage and related services. Table 1-1[11] indicates that in 1972 those factors of production collectively accounted for 66.6 percent of the costs of NYSE member firms. While the expenditure for back office help can be regarded as variable, stock broker expense is partially fixed due to the investment of firms in preparing their registered representatives. Office costs are, of course, fixed also. Because the industry is characterized by widely varying levels of demand, fixed factors often constrain broker earnings.[12] In later stages of this study the fixed nature of certain costs will appear as a possible determinant of the conduct of brokerage operations.

Other Activities

Brokerage firms engage in several activities in addition to providing securities brokerage and related customer services. For example, to enable customers to buy more stock than they otherwise could, firms lend clients a portion of the cost of security purchases. The terms of

Table 1-1
Relative Factor Costs of NYSE Firms

	1970	1971	1972
Registered Representatives	18.5%	22.1%	22.3%
Back Office Personnel	29.1	28.2	26.5
Brokerage Offices	19.0	17.8	17.8
Interest	12.1	9.5	11.4
Promotional	3.6	3.5	3.5
Other Variable	9.0	9.6	9.5
Other Fixed	8.7	9.3	9.1

such margin loans are established jointly by the firms, the New York Stock Exchange, and the Board of Governors of the Federal Reserve System. To finance margin activities brokerage houses borrow large sums from banks using their customers' securities as collateral. They earn the one percent difference between the rate charged by banks and the rate they charge their customers. In recent years, between thirty and forty percent of stock purchases made by the public have involved margin loans. On June 30, 1972, customers of firms belonging to the New York Stock Exchange had debit margin balances of 7.8 billion dollars.[13] This represents annual income to the industry of between $70 and $80 million.

Many brokerage houses trade securities for their own account. Acting as principals, the companies advertise "bid" prices at which they will buy and "asked" prices at which they will sell specific securities. The return of such market making activities arises from the difference between the bid and asked prices as well as the capital gains and losses associated with carrying an inventory of stocks. Firms finance their inventories through bank loans principally secured by stocks held in their customer's margin accounts.[14] In this activity, brokerage houses function like exchange specialists with the exception that they compete with other market makers. Markets are made in approximately 40,000 issues, with one firm dealing in from 20 to 1500 different securities.[15]

Underwriting new stock and bond issues is another source of revenue to the industry. Underwriting brokers first negotiate with companies intending to raise capital. Upon establishing the terms under which the new securities will be brought to the market, underwriters register the offering with the SEC. They subsequently publish a prospectus containing information pertinent to the offering. The final task is to arrange public sale and distribution of the securities through a syndicate of brokerage houses. For this service, brokerage firms receive as much as fifteen percent of the capital they raise, making underwriting a lucrative field. However, because many new equity issues can only be brought to the market in periods of stock market strength, levels of underwriting activity are highly variable. In 1969, stocks and bonds worth $82.5 billion came to the market for the first time. This compares with underwritings worth only $62.5 billion three years later.[16]

In the last twenty-five years the brokerage industry has depended upon revenues from mutual fund sales. While one of the largest firms formed its own mutual fund, most brokers sell funds managed by companies outside the brokerage industry. The volume of fund sales is small when compared with the value of stock transactions. However, this activity represents a significant contribution to industry revenues since the 9.3% effective commission rate on most funds is from four to five times greater than the typical charge on stock transactions.[17] Like many broker activities, mutual fund sales depend upon the performance of the stock market.

Finally, brokerage houses sell commodities, real estate participations, tax shelters, and life insurance. While commissions on commodities futures have constituted between 1.5 and 3.0 percent of industry revenue for many years,[18] real estate, tax, and insurance programs are new innovations. Many brokerage houses have promoted these devices to reduce their dependence on stock market fluctuations. To date, they have contributed a small portion of total industry sales.[19]

Table 1-2 indicates that security commissions are the largest source of revenue to firms holding membership in the New York Stock Exchange.[20] Market making and underwriting are of secondary importance. The gross revenue figures overstate the significance of margin activity since brokerage houses remit most margin income to creditor banks. The relative importance of these sources of revenue to industry profit has not been assessed. However, the nature of brokerage operations makes it clear that firms are able to make margin loans, trade stocks, underwrite securities, and sell mutual funds largely because they are the buying and selling agents of thirty million stock owners.[21] This study will focus on the broker function and related customer services, viewing other activities as ancillary

Table 1-2
Relative Sources of Revenue to NYSE Firms

Source	1970	1971	1972
Security Commissions	52.9%	54.9%	52.9%
Margin	9.6	6.6	9.8
Market Making	14.3	14.0	12.7
Underwriting	12.0	14.8	12.9
Mutual Fund Sales	2.0	1.9	1.7
Commodity Commissions	2.2	1.7	2.6
Other	7.0	6.0	7.4

areas of firm operation which arise from the broker's primary position as a buying and selling agent.

Conclusions

1. Firms in the brokerage industry provide a service: buying and selling securities as agents for the public.

2. Registered representatives act primarily as brokerage salesmen. Working closely with customers, they are the client's strongest link with a brokerage firm. Other brokerage functions are performed by back office employees.

3. In connection with the sales function, brokers and nonbroker employees extend a variety of free services to brokerage customers. Brokerage offices also afford customers many investment-related services.

4. Registered representatives, back office staff members, and brokerage offices are the industry's principal factors of production. Due to the substantial investment in training brokers, part of the cost associated with this factor is fixed as is office expense.

5. While industry participants engage in a number of other activities, securities brokerage is their primary business.

2 Organization of the Industry

[The exchange] was in no mood for new members. It had become, in great measure, an exclusive club, a situation of which the brokers were very proud. They wore silk hats and swallowtail coats during business hours. It was a genteel business as well as a profitable one. The entry of young men was frowned upon. To this end, initiation fees were raised to $1,000, a hard fact which kept many young men from joining the organization, even when they were able to overcome the hurdle of five blackballs for membership.

– The New York Stock Exchange, 1858

The New York Stock Exchange has been central in the structure of the brokerage industry. Owned by 517 of the largest brokerage firms, the Exchange has provided a means through which industry participants can coordinate entry and pricing policies. This has been accomplished with a low degree of industrial concentration.

The New York Stock Exchange

In the United States more than sixty percent of brokerage transactions are executed on organized exchanges.[1] Of these, approximately ninety percent involve the two national stock exchanges, the New York Stock Exchange (NYSE) and the American Stock Exchange (ASE). Twelve regional stock exchanges account for the remainder. Those markets originally dealt in securities issued by local companies. However, with the advent of modern communications systems regional markets now deal primarily in stocks listed on the NYSE.[2] The equity instruments of many small companies are not traded on any exchange. Instead, brokerage houses in various cities trade such "unlisted" stocks using the telephone in the over-the-counter market. The relative importance of listed and unlisted securities to participants in the brokerage industry is indicated by

G.L. Leffler and L.C. Farwell, *The Stock Market*, p. 94.

Table 2-1.[3] Exchange transactions represent an average of 92.1 percent of the commission revenue received by the twelve NYSE member firms that have made such data public.

In order to trade stocks on an exchange, a firm must own an exchange membership or "seat." Ownership of a seat entitles the member firm to have one representative on the floor of the exchange executing orders for the firm's customers. In the case of the New York Stock Exchange, membership also imposes certain restrictions. For example, member firms are required to maintain a minimum net capital of $60,000. They contribute one percent of their commissions to support the administration of the Exchange.[4] Most importantly, members must respect Exchange policies in the conduct of their business. The influence of those policies on competitive practices within the industry will be examined in later chapters.

Firms that are not members of the NYSE lack access to the floor of the Exchange. However, they often trade New York listed securities over the counter in what is called the Third Market. The majority of such transactions are large orders placed by financial institutions. Third Market trading represents less than ten percent of

Table 2-1
Listed and Unlisted Commission Revenue (1971)

Firm	Securities Commission (Millions)	Percent Listed	Percent Unlisted
Merrill, Lynch, Pierce, Fenner and Smith	$361.2	95.2%	4.8%
Bache and Co.	86.1	90.5	9.5
E.F. Hutton and Co.	81.7	90.9	9.1
Dean Witter and Co.	81.2	92.7	7.3
Paine, Webber, Jackson and Curtis	65.3	90.2	9.8
Reynolds Securities	41.0	89.9	10.1
CBWL-Hayden, Stone	27.5	88.6	11.4
Mitchum, Jones and Templeton	27.2	80.4	19.6
A.G. Edwards and Sons	20.7	80.7	19.3
Piper Jaffray and Hopwood	7.3	82.9	17.1
Jas H. Oliphant and Co.	6.3	96.8	3.2
First of Michigan Corp.	3.6	90.1	9.9
Average (weighted by commission revenue)		92.1%	7.9%

all activity in NYSE listed stocks.[5] At times financial institutions trade with each other without the services of a broker. These transactions comprise the Fourth Market. Although each trade is usually large, Fourth Market transactions in the aggregate represent a negligible proportion of securities volume.[6]

For several reasons the NYSE is regarded as the nation's primary equity market. First, transactions on the regional exchanges and in the Third and Fourth Markets usually take place at or near the prevailing New York price. Also, firms that list securities on the Exchange are among the oldest and largest companies in the country. The fact that NYSE transactions have been subject to public scrutiny and Federal regulation for forty years contributes to investor confidence in the brokerage services of Exchange member firms.[7] Because tens of thousands of investors follow NYSE transactions moment by moment, the Exchange provides a continuous auction market that is able to absorb relatively large orders at almost any time. This offers stock holders a degree of liquidity found in few other investments. Finally, due to the Exchange's large volume and central role, the spread between the bid and asked prices of listed securities is narrower than in other markets.[8] By reducing transactions costs, this further enhances the appeal of NYSE brokerage services.

Table 2-2[9] reflects the dominance of the NYSE. As measured by the value of common stock transactions on organized exchanges, between seventy-eight and eighty-six percent of brokerage services involve the Exchange. While it has lost some ground to the ASE, the NYSE continues to trade about eight times as much stock as any other exchange. Accordingly, the Exchange is the most important source of commissions to the brokerage industry.[10] This study of the brokerage industry is primarily concerned with brokerage on the New York Stock Exchange.

Market Entry

The number of seats on the NYSE is fixed at 1366. Approximately 1100 of these are held by commission brokers who execute orders for member firms.[11] To handle their greater volume, several large firms control more than one seat. Commission brokers affiliated with brokerage houses are assisted by unaffiliated ("two-dollar") commis-

Table 2-2
Dollar Volume by Exchange

	Volume ($billions)	NYSE %	ASE %	Midwest %	Pacific %	Other Regional %
1935	15.4	86.6	7.8	1.3	1.4	2.9
1940	8.4	85.2	7.7	2.1	1.5	3.5
1945	16.3	82.8	10.8	2.0	1.8	2.6
1950	21.8	85.9	6.9	2.4	2.2	2.6
1955	38.0	86.3	7.0	2.4	1.9	2.4
1960	45.3	83.8	9.4	2.7	1.9	2.2
1965	89.5	81.8	9.9	3.4	2.4	2.5
1970	131.7	78.5	11.1	3.7	3.8	2.9
1971	186.4	79.1	10.0	4.0	3.8	3.1

sion brokers who charge brokerage firms a flat fee for every transaction they handle. Other seats are owned by Exchange specialists who provide a ready market when an order received by a commission broker cannot be otherwise executed. A small number of seats are held by oddlot dealers who execute portions of orders that are not multiples of one hundred shares, the standard unit in which securities are traded. Floor brokers, who trade for their own accounts as private agents, control about thirty seats.[12] The seats owned by specialists, oddlot dealers, and floor traders seldom change hands.

Because a firm has to own a membership in order to trade on the Exchange, companies contemplating entrance to the industry must buy seats from existing commission brokers. Thus, the emergence of a new market participant in general requires exit by an established one. This diminishes the threat of market entry as a competitive influence among existing brokerage houses. That is, should Exchange policies yield persistent super-normal returns, entry by new competitors will not reduce the level of sales per firm since the number of firms cannot substantially rise. In the words of George Stigler, there is "an absence of free entry . . .[because] the seats of the New York Stock Exchange members are fixed in number."[13] Entry is further restricted by the use of "tests, fees, blackballs, investigations of character, and income and asset requirements" directed toward potential new members.[14] Moreover, as the largest users of brokerage services, banks, insurance companies, and mutual funds are logical potential market entrants. Yet under Exchange rules, financial institutions have been explicitly prevented from owning seats in the past.[15] To illustrate the height of the resulting barriers to entry, Allan Meltzer points out that during a period (1945-1962) in which Exchange volume increased by 350 percent, the number of NYSE member firms increased by only 15 percent.[16]

The Price of NYSE Membership

Due to varying business conditions and the deaths of members, NYSE seats periodically change hands. Table 2-3[17] indicates the high and low prices at which Exchange memberships have been traded in selected years. The figures shown are adjusted for an increase in the number of seats in 1929.[18] Figure 2-1 represents the median value of seats in both current and constant dollars. The figure indicates that seat prices were especially high in the late 1920s and, to a lesser extent, in the late 1960s. During the periods 1927-1931 and 1965-1969 the average price of seats was respectively $718,000 and $323,000 (1968 dollars). These levels have been equaled in no other period. During the first five months of 1974 seats traded for between $80,000 and $95,000.[19]

The price of memberships is related to earnings within the industry. Any company that contemplates buying a seat would clearly pay no more than the expected return of participating in NYSE brokerage. Nor would a brokerage house owning a seat be induced to sell it for less. It is therefore reasonable that the value of NYSE seats capitalizes the expected profit of member firms.[20] The record level of seat prices in the late 1920s tends to confirm this hypothesis since those years are generally acknowledged to be the most profitable in this century.[21] In the same way, an increase in the price of seats was associated with higher industry earnings during the late 1960s.[22] For the period 1926-1965 Robert Doede has rigorously demonstrated the proposition that membership prices capitalize broker earnings. In his 1967 dissertation,[23] Doede develops a complex expectations model under the assumption that industry profit is a constant proportion of Exchange volume. His empirical tests confirm the hypothesis that seat prices are determined by capitalizing the expected value of the economic profit accruing to

Table 2-3
The Price of Seats on the NYSE ($Thousands)

Year	High Price	Low Price
1900	47.5	37.5
1901	80.0	48.5
1902	81.0	65.0
1903	82.0	51.0
1904	81.0	57.0
1905	85.0	72.0
1906	95.0	78.0
1907	88.0	51.0
1908	80.0	51.0
1909	94.0	73.0
1910	94.0	65.0
1911	73.0	65.0
1912	74.0	55.0
1913	53.0	37.0
1914	55.0	34.0
1915	74.0	38.0
1916	76.0	60.0
1917	77.0	45.0
1918	60.0	45.0
1919	110.0	60.0
1920	115.0	85.0
1921	100.0	77.5
1922	100.0	86.0
1923	100.0	76.0
1924	101.0	76.0
1925	150.0	99.0
1926	175.0	133.0
1927	305.0	170.0
1928	595.0	290.0
1929	495.0	350.0
1930	480.0	205.0
1931	322.0	125.0
1932	185.0	68.0
1933	259.0	90.0
1934	190.0	70.0
1935	140.0	65.0
1936	174.0	89.0
1937	134.0	61.0
1938	85.0	51.0
1939	70.0	51.0
1940	60.0	33.0

Table 2-3 (cont.)

Year	High Price	Low Price
1941	35.0	19.0
1942	30.0	17.0
1943	48.0	27.0
1944	75.0	40.0
1945	95.0	49.0
1946	97.0	61.0
1947	70.0	50.0
1948	68.0	46.0
1949	49.0	35.0
1950	54.0	46.0
1951	68.0	52.0
1952	55.0	39.0
1953	60.0	38.0
1954	88.0	45.0
1955	90.0	80.0
1956	113.0	75.0
1957	89.0	65.0
1958	127.0	69.0
1959	157.0	110.0
1960	162.0	135.0
1961	225.0	147.0
1962	210.0	115.0
1963	217.0	160.0
1964	230.0	190.0
1965	250.0	190.0
1966	270.0	197.0
1967	450.0	220.0
1968	550.0	385.0
1969	515.0	260.0
1970	320.0	130.0
1971	300.0	145.0
1972	250.0	150.0

NYSE member firms. This result will prove useful in later stages of the present study.

Industry Concentration

As measured by market concentration, the industry selling brokerage service on the New York Stock Exchange exhibits a competitive

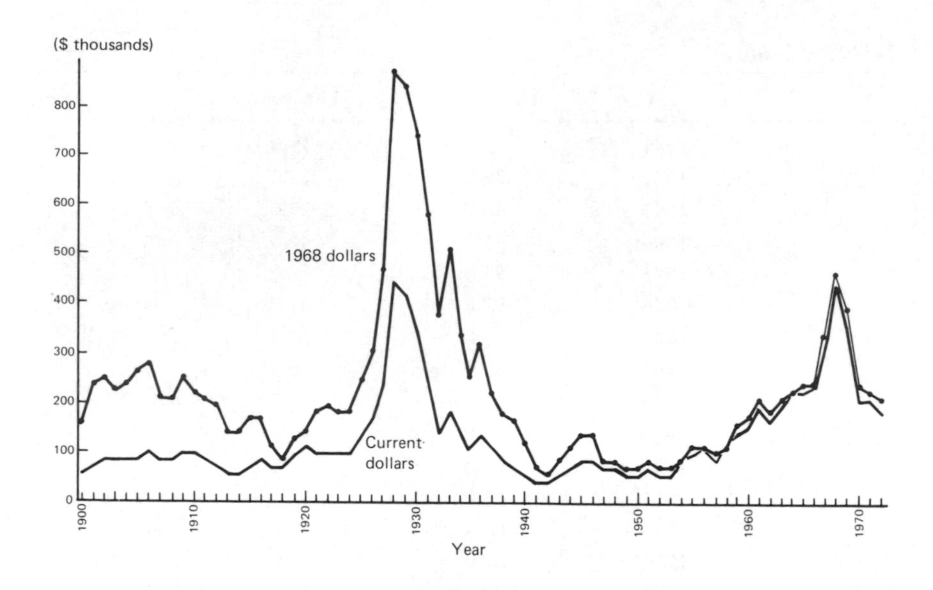

Figure 2-1. Median NYSE Seat Prices

industrial structure. In each of their ancillary activities, brokerage houses compete with thousands of more specialized firms. For example, most banks issue loans for the purchase of stocks.[24] These differ from margin loans in name only. In the same way, the 517 member firms face competition in market making activities from the 4176 nonmember broker-dealers registered with the Securities and Exchange Commission.[25] The rival broker-dealers also engage in commodity and mutual fund sales. In underwriting new securities offerings, NYSE firms compete with banks and specialized investment banking houses. Finally, a large number of independent agents sell tax shelter programs and life insurance policies similar to those sold by brokerage houses.

It appears that the industry's primary activity, brokerage in NYSE listed securities, is also relatively unconcentrated. Unfortunately, the Exchange has not published the market shares attributable to each member firm. However, in a study unrelated to market concentration,[26] the Exchange released enlightening figures about the number of transactions executed in 1966 by groups of firms of different size. As reported in Table 2-4, these permit some inferences about the concentration of brokerage operations. The data indicate that the

Table 2-4
Market Concentration among NYSE Firms (1966)

	Exchange Data		Calculated Data			
Class[b]	Number of Firms in Class	Average Transactions Per Firm[a]	Total Number of Transactions in Class[a]	Cumulative Number of Transactions[a]	Cumulative Number of Firms	Concentration Ratio (%)
1	2	3.800	7.600	7.600	2	16.8
2	7	1.250	8.750	16.350	9	36.1
3	9	0.735	6.615	22.965	18	50.8
4	24	0.306	7.344	30.309	42	67.0
5	46	0.143	6.578	36.887	88	81.5
6	78	0.063	4.914	41.801	166	92.4

Total number of transactions: 45.240 million.

[a]In millions.

[b]By decreasing firm size.

largest nine NYSE firms handle about 36.1 percent of the transactions. The estimated eighteen-firm concentration ratio is 50.8 percent. These figures represent a relatively low degree of concentration since an eight-firm ratio of seventy percent is often cited as the benchmark denoting above average concentration. Indeed, the *eighteen*-firm figure for the brokerage industry is substantially lower than a majority of *eight*-firm concentration ratios of representative four- and five-digit industries calculated in a 1963 Senate study.[27] It appears that a low degree of concentration characterizes all areas of brokerage activity.

Conclusions

1. Brokerage services on the New York Stock Exchange represent the most important source of revenue to the industry.

2. The fixed number of seats on the NYSE restricts entry into the brokerage industry as does the rule limiting membership by financial institutions.

3. The price of Exchange memberships capitalizes profits accruing to industry participants.

4. All areas of brokerage house activity are characterized by low levels of industrial concentration.

Part II: Conduct of the Brokerage Business

3 Noncompetitive Pricing

We, the subscribers, brokers for the purchase and sale of public stocks, do hereby solemnly promise and pledge ourselves to each other that we will not buy or sell from this date, for any person whatsoever, any kind of public stocks at a less rate than one-quarter of one per cent commission on the specie value and that we will give preference to each other in our negotiations.

–The Buttonwood Tree Agreement

Since 1792 participants in the brokerage industry have been committed to the principle of fixed commission rates. That founding principle has been embodied into the New York Stock Exchange Constitution:

On business for parties not members of the Exchange . . . the commission shall be not less than one-eighth of one per cent.[1]

While many policies have undergone change over the years, the Exchange's tradition of price collusion has not been substantially altered.

Determination of Commission Rates

The power to propose commission rate changes lies with the Board of Governors of the Exchange. The Board is composed of thirty-three persons, twenty-two of whom are elected solely by member brokerage houses. Because commission rates are stated explicitly in Article XV of the Exchange Constitution, commission rate revisions must be submitted to the entire membership for approval. Once adopted, all Exchange members are required to charge customers the collusively established schedule of prices.

The rates prescribed by the Exchange are technically the minimum fees that a member may charge on NYSE transactions. In practice,

R. Sobel, *The Big Board*, p. 21.

though, the minimum fees have been accepted as actual rates by all member firms for their NYSE, ASE, regional stock exchange, and over-the-counter brokerage operations. In addition, most nonmember brokerage houses employ the New York commission rate schedule.[2] This compounds the influence of price collusion by NYSE firms.

Exchange pricing policy has been objected to by some of the large, nationwide member firms. In particular, those firms that aggressively seek the accounts of small customers have opposed fee increases in the past.[3] One sizeable firm contends that fixed commission rates should be abolished altogether.[4] However, the large houses control few seats in relation to the volume of business they execute. About half of all NYSE transactions are originated by firms owning only seven percent of the memberships.[5] For this reason, large firms have had little influence in proposing and establishing commission rate changes. Instead, NYSE price policy has been guided by smaller firms which operate only one or two offices. Exchange research indicates that these houses are less efficient than their nationwide counterparts.[6]

The Exchange has in the past cited rising costs as the reason for revising the commission schedule. According to the Board of Governors, increased communications and wage costs in the brokerage industry led to the 1919 rise.[7] In 1924 a rate increase was said to be "a further reflection of the cost handicaps under which brokerage houses have been doing business and which have likewise tended to restrict their operations."[8] On still another occasion, a NYSE Special Committee on Commissions concluded that "Commission revenue has fallen below the cost of handling a transaction in spite of efforts to introduce economy."[9] These pronouncements notwithstanding, the Exchange made no attempt before 1968 to identify the average or marginal costs of processing transactions.[10] A detailed understanding of the industry cost structure would seem to be especially important to establish the relative commissions on orders of different size.[11] It would also shed more light on the comparative efficiency of large and small firms.

Enforcement

To maintain its fixed pricing structure, the Exchange enforces several policies which prevent price shading among members. It has explicitly prohibited any form of direct rebate in Section 1 of Article XV of the Exchange Constitution:

> Commissions shall be charged and paid, under all circumstances, upon all purchases or sales of securities dealt in upon the Exchange; and shall be absolutely net and free from all or any rebatement, return, discount or allowance in any shape or manner whatsoever, or by any method or arrangement.[12]

In addition, Rule 394 provides that members may not trade NYSE listed stocks off the Exchange. Thus, member firms are excluded from the Third Market, where competitive commissions prevail. To insure that these rules are respected by all firms, brokerage houses acting collectively through the NYSE have stipulated the stiffest of penalties for violators: denial of access to the Exchange floor. Whereas the Constitution calls for fines for most other violations,[13] in relation to commission rate infractions it states:

> If the Governing Board shall determine that a member of the Exchange has violated the provisions of this Article, it shall suspend such member, for the first offense, for such period not less than one year and not more than five years . . . A member adjudged guilty of a second offense . . . shall be expelled by a like vote.[14]

These penalties have been sufficient to prevent price shading. A search of the *Wall Street Journal* and a recent history of the Exchange reveals only one incident of commission discounting.[15] Since a round of price cutting in the late 1920s, the commission rate schedule has been respected by all member firms.

The Third Market

The adherence of NYSE members to the fixed commission structure has led many nonmembers to trade listed stocks over the counter in the Third Market. As was suggested in Chapter 1, that market has traditionally served financial institutions that would otherwise be forced to pay the same commission per share as individual investors pay on their small orders. In response to institutional needs, Third Market "block houses" have become especially adept at handling very large orders. In the last three years, Third Market brokers have also solicited business from the public. Individual investors receive commission discounts, which vary with the size and, in some instances, frequency of orders. Savings of from twenty to fifty-six percent are realized on representative round lot transactions.[16] However, Third Market dealers do not extend the customer services that NYSE members furnish. Indeed, most dealers lack both registered representatives and board rooms. As a result, the Third Market does not appeal to all investors.[17] According to SEC figures[18] shown in Table 3-1, that market represents a small fraction of all transactions in New York listed securities. While the Third Market enjoyed substantial growth between 1965 and 1972, that trend has not continued.

Recently the Exchange has offered commission discounts on large orders to attract institutional customers away from the Third Market. At the direction of the Securities and Exchange Commission, brokerage fees now must be negotiated between broker and customer on that part of a transaction which is worth more than $300,000. However, this affects very few orders. The largest and second largest brokerage firms estimate that such transactions represent only 2.7 and 1.8 percent of their commission business, respectively.[19] Thus, collusively established brokerage rates still dominate.

The Level of Brokerage Rates

The success of Exchange members in fixing prices is perhaps best measured by the historical trend of commission rates. However, several problems arise in developing an index of brokerage fees. First, the NYSE round lot commission schedule is based on the dollar value of the stock to be traded. In order to fully capture changes in that schedule, an index of commission rates would have to be derived from the brokerage fees associated with orders of different size. Unfortunately, little information is available on the size distribution of Exchange transactions, making it difficult to weight such an index. In addition, the general price level and the price of stocks should be considered. The fact that most prices have risen over time suggests that changes in the (nominal) level of NYSE commission rates overstate the success of brokerage firms in colluding to raise their fees. At the same time, it must be realized that rising stock prices have effectively increased the commissions on brokerage transactions.[20]

Table 3-1
Third Market Volume in Stocks Listed on the NYSE as a Proportion of NYSE Volume

Year	Quarter	Shares	Dollar Volume
1965	1	3.1%	4.1%
	2	2.8	3.5
	3	2.7	3.4
	4	2.3	2.9
1966	1	2.5	2.9
	2	2.4	2.8
	3	2.8	2.9
	4	2.9	3.2
1967	1	2.7	3.1
	2	3.0	3.3
	3	3.0	3.3
	4	3.1	3.4
1968	1	3.5	3.9
	2	3.2	3.6
	3	3.6	4.4
	4	4.2	4.7
1969	1	4.0	4.7
	2	4.5	5.1
	3	5.4	5.8
	4	5.7	6.4
1970	1	6.4	7.2
	2	5.9	6.9
	3	6.7	8.5
	4	7.0	8.6
1971	1	6.3	8.3
	2	6.8	7.9
	3	7.2	8.3
	4	7.8	9.3
1972	1	7.2	8.6
	2	7.8	9.0
	3	8.3	9.1
	4	6.1	7.4
1973	1	6.4	7.3
	2	5.9	7.2
	3	5.3	6.6
	4	5.4	6.6

In order to deal with these complications, two indicators are adopted to illustrate the historical trend of NYSE commission rates. The first index, used extensively in later chapters, is the commission on a round lot transaction involving fifty-dollar-per-share stock. This representative $5000 transaction approximates the average size of round lot trades as reported by the NYSE.[21] The second column of Table 3-2 reports the brokerage fee associated with the representative transaction for every year since 1900. The data indicate that brokerage fees have risen substantially since the mid-1930s. From 1935 to 1972 the fee associated with the $5000 round lot transaction climbed from $17.50 to $67.00. Stated alternatively, the transactions cost of trading the asset has increased from 0.35 to 1.34 percent of its value. This near quadrupling of commission rates compares with a 250 percent rise in the general price level. Thus, this measure indicates that brokerage fees have increased half again as fast as other prices.

For purposes of illustration, the figures in the second column of Table 3-2 have in the third column been deflated by the ratio of a wholesale price index and a stock price index (1967 = 100).[22] This adjusted measure of brokerage rates accounts for the effects of inflation and changing stock prices. Since the turn of the century, it has risen more than three times as fast as the unadjusted rate. This reflects the fact that securities asset prices, on which commissions are based, have moved faster than the general price level. The figures indicate that the unadjusted commission on the representative transaction tends to understate the rate at which brokerage fees have been raised. Due to the structure of the New York Stock Exchange commission schedule, the brokerage industry has clearly been a beneficiary of rising stock prices.

Figure 3-1 illustrates that by either of the two measures, the fees charged by brokers have risen dramatically since the mid-1930s. The data collectively suggest that Exchange member firms have broadly exercised the price discretion they possess. However, at this point it is not clear whether rapidly rising brokerage rates can be attributed solely to Exchange monopoly power. The effects of federal regulation and improved customer service on brokerage fees have yet to be assessed.

Conclusions

1. Acting through the NYSE, brokerage firms have been able to establish common prices that are respected throughout the industry.

Table 3-2
NYSE Commission Rates since 1900

Year	Rate	Adjusted Rate
1900	$12.50	$3.63
1901	12.50	3.74
1902	12.50	3.76
1903	12.50	3.19
1904	12.50	3.11
1905	12.50	3.94
1906	12.50	4.10
1907	12.50	3.17
1908	12.50	3.26
1909	12.50	3.79
1910	12.50	3.50
1911	12.50	3.75
1912	12.50	3.63
1913	12.50	3.21
1914	12.50	3.13
1915	12.50	3.15
1916	12.50	2.91
1917	12.50	1.90
1918	12.50	1.51
1919	15.00	2.00
1920	15.00	1.63
1921	15.00	2.22
1922	15.00	2.75
1923	15.00	2.69
1924	15.00	2.91
1925	17.50	3.97
1926	17.50	4.64
1927	17.50	5.93
1928	17.50	7.62
1929	17.50	10.08
1930	17.50	8.97
1931	17.50	6.91
1932	17.50	3.92
1933	17.50	5.01
1934	17.50	4.85
1935	17.50	4.88
1936	17.50	7.06
1937	17.50	6.59
1938	18.00	5.55
1939	18.00	5.93
1940	18.00	5.32

Table 3-2 (cont.)

Year	Rate	Adjusted Rate
1941	18.00	4.26
1942	25.00	4.63
1943	25.00	5.86
1944	25.00	6.32
1945	25.00	7.55
1946	25.00	7.45
1947	25.00	5.39
1948	31.00	6.32
1949	31.00	6.52
1950	31.00	7.58
1951	31.00	8.26
1952	31.00	9.32
1953	31.00	9.54
1954	40.00	14.74
1955	40.00	20.06
1956	40.00	20.44
1957	40.00	20.69
1958	44.00	23.39
1959	44.00	28.96
1960	44.00	29.16
1961	44.00	33.56
1962	44.00	31.49
1963	44.00	35.38
1964	44.00	41.12
1965	44.00	43.68
1966	44.00	40.88
1967	44.00	44.00
1968	44.00	46.08
1969	44.00	43.97
1970	44.00	36.07
1971	44.00	41.30
1972	67.00	68.02

2. In the past, rate increases have been initiated by the smaller, less efficient firms that control Exchange pricing policy. Usually fee raises have been attributed to higher costs.

3. To enforce its price fixing agreement, the Exchange has adopted measures which would exclude violators from trading on the NYSE. With one exception during 1929, members have not shaded their prices.

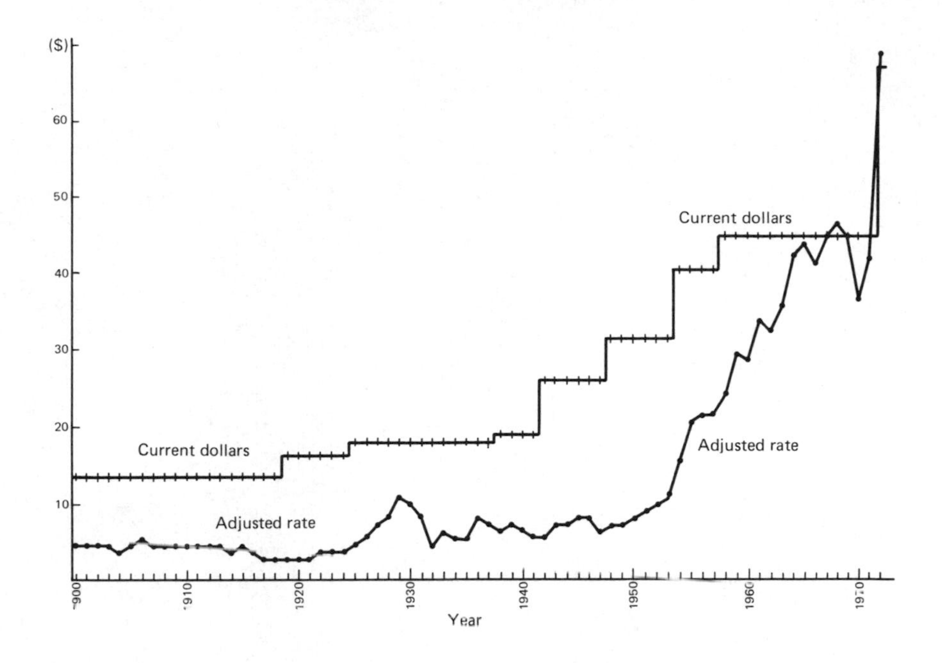

Figure 3-1. NYSE Commission Rates

4. Price competition exists in the Third Market, which serves institutional and individual investors. On the representative round lot transaction, investors may receive a commission discount of from twenty to fifty-six percent in that market.

5. Despite the emergence of the Third Market and negotiated commissions on large orders, the NYSE heritage of price fixing remains substantially intact.

6. In the last forty years, commission rates have risen fifty percent faster than other prices.

4 Regulation

It is doubtful whether any other type of public regulation of economic activity has been so widely admired as regulation of the securities markets by the Securities and Exchange Commission.

– George Stigler

The American experience with regulation, despite notable achievements, has had its disappointing aspects. Regulation has too often resulted in protection of the status quo. *Entry is often blocked, prices are kept from falling, and the industry becomes inflexible and insensitive to new techniques and opportunities for progress.*

– Economic Report of the President, 1970

The speculative excesses that led to the failure of the stock market in 1929 moved New Deal administrators to conclude that the American securities markets were in need of reform.[1] The resulting legislation placed both the securities markets and the industry servicing them under the supervision of the Securities and Exchange Commission. From an economic point of view, much of the Commission's policy can only be explained by its dual role: regulation of the *investments markets* through full disclosure, prevention of price manipulation, and limitation of stock market credit; and overseeing the *brokerage industry* through registration and supervision of brokerage firms and the exchanges. Because the SEC was created in response to the failure of the securities markets, the Commission appears to have been primarily concerned with the performance of that market. Conditions in the market for brokerage services have received less attention.[2] Regulation of the brokerage business is distinguished by the fact that its *raison d'etre* is not related to competitive characteristics of the industry itself.

George J. Stigler, "Public Regulation of the Securities Markets' Operations," *Journal of Business*, Vol. 37, April 1964, p. 117.
Economic Report of the President, 1970, pp. 107, 108.

Industry Self-Regulation

The Securities Exchange Act of 1934 provides for brokerage industry "self-regulation," a unique form of federal supervision. That principle recognizes that between 1792 and 1934 the industry was operated much like a private club with exclusive jurisdiction over its members.[3] Accordingly, under self-regulation the SEC has delegated certain supervisory duties to the exchanges. The Commission intervenes only when serious violations of the securities acts have occurred or when it perceives that the policies of the exchanges work contrary to the public interest. In the view of a former SEC chairman, self-regulation lets

> the exchanges take the leadership with government playing a residual role. Government would keep the shotgun behind the door, loaded, well oiled, cleaned, ready for use but with the hope that it would never have to be used.[4]

The SEC has shown particular hesitancy to challenge New York Stock Exchange pricing and entry policies. This has been an important determinant of conduct within the brokerage industry.

As embodied in the Securities Exchange Act, the concept of self-regulation appears to envision continuation of collusive pricing by NYSE members. The legislation indirectly establishes the legitimacy of Exchange price fixing where it refers to SEC authority "to alter or supplement the rules" of the Exchange when necessary "in respect to such matters as . . . the fixing of reasonable rates of commission."[5] Drafted in the era of the *Appalachian Coals* decision and the National Industrial Recovery Act, the bill sanctions noncompetitive pricing behavior among brokerage houses. More recently, industry pricing policy was examined in the 3000-page SEC *Special Study*. Summarizing the Commission's findings, it states:

> Th[is] report demonstrates that neither the fundamental structure of the securities markets nor the regulatory pattern of the securities acts requires dramatic reconstruction.[6]

This has been widely interpreted as an endorsement by the Commission of self-regulation in its traditional dimensions.[7]

Under the SEC, the principle of self-regulation has insulated the industry from antitrust action. In the 1963 *Silver vs. the NYSE* case, it was argued that by ordering a member to cease ticker service to the nonmember plaintiff, the Exchange was guilty of a group boycott which is illegal *per se* under the antitrust statutes.[8] The Supreme Court upheld Silver's suit since the SEC had not acted in the matter. This established the very important precedent that antitrust laws are not applicable where the Commission exercises its authority to reconcile the aim of protecting competition with the effective operation of the securities markets. In particular, the *Silver* precedent was extended to include Exchange pricing policy by the *Kaplan vs. Lehman Brothers* decision. In that case, the plaintiff charged that the fixed commission rate structure violates Section 1 of the Sherman Act as a price fixing conspiracy. The High Court found in favor of the member firm because the SEC has supervised rate setting under authority granted by the 1934 act.[9] Through an *amicus curiae* brief, the SEC urged affirmance of this principle.[10] Exchange entry policies have been similarly vindicated. In *Thill Securities vs. the NYSE*, the Circuit Court of Appeals stated that the Sherman Act is not applicable where, "Beyond the mere possibility of SEC review," it is demonstrated that the Commission is in fact "exercising actual and adequate review" of Exchange policies. Finding that appropriate review of entry policies had taken place, the Court upheld NYSE rules which deny nonmembers access to the floor of the Exchange.[11] The obvious thrust of the *Silver, Kaplan*, and *Thill* decisions is that SEC regulation insulates industry policies from antitrust prosecution.[12] In the view of the SEC *Special Study* Economist,

> Any immunity from antitrust action in the securities field that may be brought on the grounds of price fixing by member firms presumably rests heavily upon the Commission's jurisdiction in this area . . .
>
> Clearly the reason for this ability of the securities business to conduct itself without the ordinary imposed direct government restraints, is the associated supervisory responsibility of the SEC . . .
>
> Under the umbrella of self regulation, uniform prices have been permitted in the securities business without antitrust action being invoked.[13]

Manifestly, Professor Stigler's precept that "The ghost of Senator Sherman is an *ex officio* member of the board of directors of every large corporation"[14] requires some amendment.

SEC Control of Commission Rates

While the SEC has protected Exchange members from antitrust regulation, the agency's own record of regulating industry price fixing practices is somewhat disappointing. Despite its charge to assure "reasonable brokerage fees," the SEC has never publicly articulated standards against which the level of commission rates could be tested. Nor has it developed a theory of the structure of rates on transactions of different size. Moreover, the SEC has proven less than formidable in its supervision of industry self-regulation. In the first thirty years of its existence, the Commission altered an Exchange rule only once on its own initiative.[15] That instance involved a minor matter unrelated to brokerage fees. Within the last few years, the Commission has exercised its broad statutory powers on a few occasions. In May of 1968, the SEC for the first time asked the NYSE to alter a rule related to commissions by giving volume discounts on very large brokerage transactions. It has also gone as far as proposing the abolition of fixed commission rates.[16] However, this adversary role is not representative of the Commission's historical posture in relation to industry pricing policy.

In the absence of federal guidelines, the Exchange made five commission rate revisions between 1935 and 1967. At various times, the SEC

> indicated some lack of enthusiasm for the changes, obtained modest revisions, and stated the need for study. Except for such occasional mildly negative reactions, the Commission . . . has never imposed any serious objection to the rate increases that have been adopted and, by and large, they have followed the form of the original proposals.[17]

The SEC has itself confirmed the independence of brokerage houses in collusively establishing their rates. Its *1968 Annual Report* opens with the observation that, "The setting of commission rates for exchange transactions is . . . [an] area in which exchanges have been permitted to establish rules of practice."[18] The SEC's acceptance of collusive pricing was reaffirmed as recently as 1972 when, as in five previous rate adjustments, the Commission advised the NYSE that it "would not object to that Exchange's implementation of a new minimum commission rate schedule."[19]

The history of commission rates bears evidence that SEC regulation has not abridged the price discretion enjoyed by Exchange member firms. Table 3-2 indicates that in the 35 years prior to the organization of the SEC, brokerage fees rose only twice. Relative to other prices, they declined by 2.1%. Presumably, brokerage firms acted in the shadow of the Sherman Act during this period. However, since the emergence of the SEC, brokerage fees have been raised six times. As a result, the commission on the representative transaction increased by 36.5 percent in real terms. Furthermore, the deflated mean commission rate during the latter period ($42.77) was about twenty percent higher than the average rate ($35.58) in pre-SEC years. Far from limiting the ability of brokerage firms to collusively establish prices, federal regulation has accompanied record high commission rates. By allowing the Exchange independently to determine brokerage fees under antitrust immunity, the SEC may have contributed to those higher rates.

Under the SEC, the NYSE has been able effectively to supplant price competition among its members. Until 1968, one industry practice, the customer directed give-up, challenged the price fixing authority of the NYSE. Due to the anti-rebate rule of the Exchange, members are prevented from offering direct remuneration to their customers in return for business. However, member brokerage houses often provided indirect rebates by giving up a portion of the commission on a large transaction to third party brokerage firms which had provided services to the customer placing the order. Since customers could "shop around" to find the member willing to rebate the largest portion of their commissions, give-ups represented an indirect form of price competition. Brokerage firms competed aggressively through give-ups, often rebating as much as sixty percent of a commission.[20] As Paul Samuelson once observed, "competition breathes asthmatically through the give-up."[21] In 1968 this vestige of price competition was abolished at the behest of the Securities and Exchange Commission. Responding to pressure from the Commission, the Exchange adopted a rule prohibiting customer directed give-ups.[22] The SEC was also responsible for the NYSE rule cited in Chapter 2 which limits entry into the brokerage industry by financial institutions.[23] This is consistent with its previously stated position that the restrictions on entry associated with Exchange membership policies furnish "protection for the public" from unscrupulous entrepreneurs.[24] Beyond insulating the NYSE from the Department of Justice, the Commission has protected industry pricing policy from Exchange members and potential members. In taking these actions, the SEC has exhibited its preoccupation with conditions in the securities markets to the detriment of competitive conditions within the industry which it regulates.

The Securities and Exchange Commission represents a classic case of regulators championing the regulated. In an important sense, self-regulation has become an umbrella under which noncompetitive pricing and entry practices have flourished in the brokerage industry.[25] Under federal regulation, NYSE brokerage has been characterized by many features of a utility: antitrust immunity, exclusive franchise, barriers to entry, and uniform pricing. Unlike public utilities, however, the brokerage industry itself has historically established the rates at which its services are sold.

Conclusions

1. Regulation of the brokerage industry arose from the failure of the securities markets in 1929. As a result, the SEC has not been primarily concerned with competitive practices within the market for securities brokerage.

2. Under the concept of industry self-regulation developed during the 1930s, federal supervision has perpetuated and protected noncompetitive pricing and entry policies among brokerage houses.

3. While the SEC has the authority to alter commission rates, it has done so infrequently. Since the Commission was founded, brokerage fees have risen markedly relative to other prices.

4. Nominal supervision of industry practices by the SEC has cloaked them with antitrust immunity.

5. By requiring the NYSE to abolish give-ups, the Commission eliminated a means of aggressive price competition in the industry. It has also acted to limit freedom of market entry.

5 Nonprice Competition

Six New Basic Leaders–*Look at the list: First come the oils with a new fuel epoch ahead of them and no readjustment to face. Motor and tobacco stocks reflect the tremendous prosperity of the country and the tendency to spend money on luxuries . . . Leather issues have been featured as never before and no one who realizes the demand for shoes the world over will criticize this selection. Shipping shares have been firm because the average buyer of stocks believes the commerce of the world will have need for the equipment and the organization of our leading mercantile companies.*

–Market Letter, 1920

While NYSE policy and federal regulation have led to uniform pricing of brokerage services, no attempt has been made to standardize the customer services that accompany the purchase and sale of securities. Accordingly, Exchange member firms offer a wide range of free services to their clients. A vital part of the sales function, these services represent inducements to investors to do business with firms offering them.

Customer Services

As a perusal of advertisements in the financial press reveals, the list of investor services grows from month to month. A very basic service of most brokerage firms is to provide information for the use of customers in analyzing the performance of securities. Information services take many forms. First, brokerage offices contain quotation boards, illuminated stock tickers, and electronic quotation machines, which display the latest prices at which stocks have been traded. In most board rooms, the Dow Jones news service or "broad tape" informs customers of news events that may influence securities

R. Sobel, *The Big Board*, p. 206.

prices. In addition, firms whose customers trade commodities often subscribe to the Reuter's commodity service. One brokerage concern maintains its own wire service to bring customers financial information.[1] Other news can be found in financial periodicals available in most brokerage offices. Using the telephone, registered representatives relay pertinent information from all these sources to customers who do not visit the board room. For those investors who perform their own securities analysis, the *Standard and Poor's* and *Moody's* statistical services provide data on stock prices, dividends, and capital structure. In recent years, a number of firms have established on-line computer systems through which customers can instantly retrieve this data on thousands of stocks.[2] These complex devices are representative of the innovations that brokerage houses have made to distinguish themselves from other firms through the services they offer.

In addition to providing basic data to customers, brokerage firms offer investment advice through several means. In board rooms investors have access to investment advisory services subscribed to by the firms. Registered representatives also offer advice on buying and selling specific securities. To guide investors who already own securities, firms employ a staff to analyze customers' portfolios for diversification and promise. Most brokerage houses publish daily or weekly market letters commenting on the state of the stock market, its expected short term direction, and the technical[3] behavior of favored stocks. These publications are distributed through the mails and branch offices. One medium-sized firm publishes over 400,000 copies daily.[4] Market letters are often supplemented by wires which advise short term traders of suggested levels to place limit and stop-loss orders for featured stocks. Brokerage firms also prepare company and industry analyses which recommend particular investment situations to customers. Fundamentally oriented, these range from reports of a few pages available to all clients to detailed analyses of more than fifty pages offered to preferred customers. While all brokerage houses provide investment advice, certain firms have built their reputations on the quality of their research services.[5]

Many firms provide complete account supervision to individuals who eschew all parts of the investment decision. This service takes two forms. A client may put funds in a discretionary account, which authorizes a stock broker to buy and sell stocks in his name. The registered representative and his firm are compensated through the brokerage commissions generated by the account. Alternatively, a customer having $25,000 or more may open a company managed account. These accounts are supervised either by staff portfolio managers or outside investment counsel employed by the brokerage firm. One house also provides managed account customers with detailed analyses of their financial status including their cash, real estate, insurance, and securities positions.[6] Managed accounts are offered on a no charge or reduced fee basis.

Investors also enjoy services associated with the offices occupied by brokerage firms. As has been mentioned, the libraries contained in brokerage offices provide several sources of investment information. Boardroom seating galleries allow customers to watch the illuminated ticker and broad tape. This is an important service to short term traders who follow the tape continually during market hours. To add to the comfort of customers, brokerage offices are usually well furnished. They are conveniently located, and, in many cases, are of distinctive design. Since the 1920s, many firms have developed a network of branch offices. Interbranch customer service is cited by brokerage houses as an advantage to travelling clients.[7] Those investors are also assisted by the industry-wide practice of paying for long distance telephone calls originated by clients and brokers.

Industry participants extend many services through their back office facilities as well. For example, absorbing transfer fees and taxes, brokerage firms will often re-register in the name of a customer securities he has received either as a gift or through inheritance. Back office employees tender customers' securities and exercise their subscription rights in cases of firm reorganization. They also hold investors' stock certificates in safekeeping without charge. In connection with this service, firms provide monthly statements relating dividend credits and security positions. In addition, they transmit proxy material and annual reports when securities are held for clients in the name of the firm. Finally, back office personnel sometimes perform banking services for customers including wiring funds, making bank deposits, cashing checks, and redeeming obligations of the United States government.

In recognition of their specialized needs, many brokerage houses have established separate departments to provide services to institutional customers. Some firms have arranged for private communications lines between these investors and their registered representatives.[8] Because insurance companies and mutual funds frequently deal in restricted securities, at least one brokerage house has recently employed traders who specialize in unregistered stock.[9] Other firms provide securities analysts who work directly with institutional customers.[10] In order to handle the large orders placed by these clients, firms are increasingly willing to buy and sell stock for institutions without full commitments for resale or repurchase of the securities. Through this customer service, institutions receive almost immediate settlement of orders at a known price. Incurring considerable risk, the brokerage firm in many cases subsequently executes the order at a less favorable price.[11] However, the commission charge most often offsets this loss. A number of firms are well known for providing such services to institutional customers.[12]

Certain other services are offered by particular houses. During the recent stock market decline a few firms sold commercial paper at close to cost, for example.[13] Their purpose in entering this market was to maintain contact with customers who were temporarily turning away from equity investments. Other firms sponsor investment classes and financial news radio broadcasts made by registered representatives for the benefit of investors. Investment seminars conducted by research oriented brokerage houses attract investors from all over the country.[14] Some brokerage customers have also received free supplementary insurance against failure of their brokerage house. Since last year, eighteen Exchange member firms have purchased coverage of $250,000 per client to augment the $50,000 Securities Investors Protection Corporation guarantee covering all brokers.[15] As is true with many innovations in the industry, the success of this customer service in attracting business has led other brokers to seek similar coverage.[16]

As the variety of available services suggests, rivalry exists between brokers in the customer services they provide. The practice of widely publicizing new services underscores the fact that brokerage firms view them as competitive inducements to attract business from other houses. Nowhere is this more apparent than in the daily advertisements in the *Wall Street Journal* announcing new research reports available on request.[17] In the same way, inauguration of such services as computer portfolio analysis, supplementary account insurance, investment classes, and branch openings are advertised in the financial media.[18] In contrast, member firm promotional material seldom focuses on the industry's primary product, stock brokerage. Nor is the price of brokerage advertised. Rather, firms compete with each other through the customer services that accompany the purchase and sale of securities.

The Dimensions of Nonprice Competition

This propensity of brokerage firms to compete through nonprice means is well recognized. For example, a *New York Times* article describes the "competitive fervor" which led firms to add and to improve branch offices in 1968 and 1969.[19] Another report cites the rivalry of brokerage houses in acquiring broker and back office employees capable of extending customer services.[20] At least one firm merged with another with the primary objective of obtaining its market research staff.[21] This type of competition apparently has its intended effect on investors. According to *Barron's*, "many institutions are choosing brokerage firms . . . by the reputation of [their] analysts" who provide customers with investment advice.[22] An industry trade journal recently used comparisons made by clients to rank NYSE member firms with respect to the quality of their research services.[23] A major brokerage house has attributed its increased share of business to its decision to offer special institutional services.[24] Speaking more generally of nonprice competition, the Chairman of a brokerage house stated that his firm's "future lies in the service we give and the advice we give, not in matching (brokerage) prices with everyone."[25] Other observers inside and outside the industry have recognized that despite their noncompetitive pricing and entry policies, brokerage firms compete vigorously through the services they offer.[26] In particular, the SEC has endorsed customer service rivalry as the acceptable form of competition between firms.[27]

While nonprice competition is a pervasive influence within the industry, it is singularly difficult to quantify. No simple measure exists of a firm's output of such things as investment advice, statistical information, and account supervision. However, some inference can be made from industry levels of factor inputs in relation to the volume of stock transactions. From Table 5-1[28] it is clear that the factor mix in the brokerage industry has varied over time. The figures indicate, for example, that between 1967 and 1969 industry expenditure on offices rose by nearly sixty percent. During the same period, stock volume increased by only three percent.

Table 5-1
Factor Costs of NYSE Firms ($Millions)

	1966	1967	1968	1969	1970	1971
Registered Representatives	507	711	945	799	619	914
Back Office Staff	586	781	1095	1161	973	1166
Brokerage Offices	348	423	568	671	636	736
Capital Costs	265	266	392	443	403	392
Advertising	82	106	141	156	120	144
Other Variable	300	419	562	366	301	399
Other Fixed	135	202	343	336	292	386
	2223	2908	4046	3932	3344	4137

Under the assumption that relative factor prices and technology did not change markedly, this suggests that customers enjoyed superior brokerage facilities in the period. Increased nonprice competition in this form was in fact noted in a contemporary report.[29] Back office and promotional expenditure similarly rose during the profitable years at the end of the 1960s, indicating that competition through back office services and advertising also increased.

Overall, the industry is estimated to spend up to fifty percent of its commission income on nonprice forms of competition.[30] This estimate is consistent with the Third Market practice of offering commission discounts of up to fifty-six percent for securities brokerage without customer services. In comparison, American laundry detergent and cigarette manufacturers report sales expenditures of thirteen and fourteen percent of revenues, respectively.[31] Both of those industries are generally regarded as exhibiting substantially above average promotional effort.[32] Thus, by conventional standards, an extensive degree of nonprice competition characterizes the conduct of the brokerage industry.

The resulting levels of customer service may exceed the needs of many investors. As was documented by the SEC, the relationships between stock owners and their brokerage houses vary considerably.[33] While some customers employ a full range of services, others use their brokers only as order-takers. For example, some clients totally ignore the advice of registered representatives, basing their investment decisions on their own analysis and privately acquired sources of information. Those people with securities holdings of more than $100,000 often employ private investment counsel, making many broker services superfluous. In some cases investors use back office services minimally, relying on their banks for stock certificate transfer and safekeeping. It is not uncommon for customers to confer with their registered representatives solely by telephone, never visiting the board rooms provided by brokerage houses. By including the cost of the full array of customer services in commission rates, brokers appear to charge some customers for products they would not otherwise buy. This possibility was raised in the SEC *Special Study*, which proposed that customer services be sold separately.[34] As yet, no brokerage house has agreed to "unbundle" its package of services.

Since April of 1974, a few large brokerage houses have experimented with "cash and carry" plans for small investors. Using these accounts, customers receive reduced service with their brokerage transactions in return for a commission discount of from fifteen to twenty-five percent.[35] While it is too early to determine the influence of these programs on industry policies, their rapid acceptance seems to substantiate that a significant portion of the investing public would prefer not to buy the assortment of services that usually accompanies the purchase and sale of securities.[36] At present, however, commission discount plans are offered by fewer than five firms and they cover a very small class of transactions.[37]

Conclusions

1. As part of the sales function, brokerage firms offer a wide variety of services to their customers.
2. Rivalry exists among firms in innovating, adopting, and publicizing customer services. This has been recognized by industry participants and regulators as a permissible means of competition within the brokerage business.
3. When examined with respect to stock volume, the factor mix employed in the industry provides an index of prevailing levels of particular types of customer service.
4. Compared with firms in other industries, NYSE member firms engage in a very high degree of nonprice competition through the services they provide.
5. Because the needs of investors vary, the SEC at one time proposed that brokerage houses unbundle their package of services. No firm has done so.

6. Evidence provided by new "cash and carry" plans suggest that many investors, when given the choice, prefer not to purchase some of the services that usually accompany brokerage transactions.

Part III: Performance within the Industry

6 The Theory of Nonprice Competition

Economic literature affords a curious mixture, confusion and separation, of the ideas of competition and monopoly. On the one hand, analysis has revealed the differences between them and has led to the perfection and refinement of a separate body of theory for each. Although the two forces are complexly interwoven, with a variety of design, throughout the price system, the fabric has been undone and refashioned into two, each more simple than the original and bearing to it only partial resemblance. Furthermore, it has, in the main, been assumed that the price system is like this—that all the phenomena to be explained are either *competitive* or *monopolistic, and therefore that the expedient of two purified and extreme types of theory is adequate.*

– Edward H. Chamberlin

Modern theoretical treatments on nonprice competition stem from the independent work of Edward Chamberlin and Joan Robinson first published in 1933. Mrs. Robinson and subsequent interpreters have emphasized that what has alternatively become known as monopolistic competition and imperfect competition arose during the financial debacle of the 1930s. It is argued that, like the Keynesian revolution in macroeconomics, the theory of nonprice competition represents a reaction to the failure of classical theories to explain widespread economic stagnation. Chamberlin, in contrast, maintains that his theory, a blending of Marshallian analysis, preceded the Great Depression.

In truth, the theoretical origins of nonprice competition predate Chamberlin and Robinson. Both Marshall and Fisher[1] mention that markets may be differentiated spacially and temporally, giving entrepreneurs limited price discretion. J.M. Clark is certainly referring to product differentiation in this passage written in 1923:

To a limited extent, each producer has his own individual market, connected more or less closely with those of his competitors, so that discrepancies are

Edward H. Chamberlin, *The Theory of Monopolistic Competition*, p. 3.

> limited in amount and in duration, becoming narrower and briefer in proportion to the standardized character of the goods.[2]

Early threads of product differentiation, like so much else, are also found in the work of F.H. Knight.[3] However, Knight and those before him discussed market fragmentation due to differences in space, time, or quality solely in the context of the perfect competition model. Piero Sraffa appears to be the first theorist to recognize the limitation of this approach. In an article[4] in 1926 he called upon theorists to "abandon the path of free competition and turn in the opposite direction, namely towards monopoly" in analyzing industry. Acknowledging the "striking parallels" between this work and his own, Chamberlin states that he was not influenced by Sraffa.[5]

Chamberlin's interest in nonprice methods of competition arose instead from the failure of contemporary economic literature to deal with trademarks.[6] In the 1920s patents were regarded as conferring monopoly power. Trademarks, though, were accepted as part of the competitive environment since their purpose is to distinguish the products of competing firms. The existence of other competitors was said to preclude the possibility of monopoly.[7] A chapter[8] written by Allyn Young led Chamberlin to the resolution of the paradoxical treatment of trademarks and patents. Young wrote that by means of a trademark an entrepreneur

> may be able to lift himself above the dead level of competition . . . [thus] he is able to obtain what might be called a quasi-monopoly. But because his power to control the price of his product is in general much more limited than that of a true monopolist, his business is more properly called competitive than monopolistic.

From this passage Chamberlin reasoned that trademarks, patents, and other sources of differentiation are at the same time monopolistic and competitive. Each is monopolistic because it makes a product unique. Each is competitive because it allows similar but not identical products. The genius of Chamberlin's theory of monopolistic competition is its recognition that most markets are characterized by both monopoly and competition, forces which had been regarded as mutually exclusive.

Monopolistic Competition

Chamberlin's 1933 book has several other distinguishing features. First, it identifies two separate sources of monopoly power: the mutual interdependence of a small number of firms and the ability of entrepreneurs to differentiate their products from those of competitors. The small numbers case, price competition between a few firms, had been dealt with by microeconomic theorists since the duopoly models of Cournot and Bertrand. However, nonprice competition through product differentiation had not previously been incorporated into models of firm behavior. Chamberlin hypothesizes that firms distinguish their products from others through

> any singularity in the quality, design, color or style . . . real or fancied, so long as it is of any importance whatever to buyers, and leads to a preference of one variety of the product over another.[9]

By differentiating their products, he argues, firms create monopoly power. This allows them limited price discretion and it tends to insulate them from the competitive responses of rival firms through price and nonprice means. In his analysis, Chamberlin regards differentiated products as entirely different goods. Thus, the productive capacity of a nation is organized not into industries but into groups of competing monopolists, each controlling completely the supply of a distinguishable product. Accordingly, Chamberlin's theory leads to an equilibrium which carries implications for the competing group as well as for individual firms. In its inception, monopolistic competition was a theory of the adjustment of nonprice competitive forces among rival firms.

The analytics associated with Chamberlin's large numbers case are well known. They rely principally upon the firm's actual demand locus *DD* and its perceived demand curve *dd* in Figure 6-1a. While *DD* embodies the reactions of other companies to changes in price by one firm, *dd* represents the quantities that could be sold by a firm if its competitors did not change their prices. Despite the presence of a large number of firms, the perceived demand curve exhibits less than perfect elasticity because each entrepreneur is able to differentiate his product from those of others. Due to the large numbers, firms act

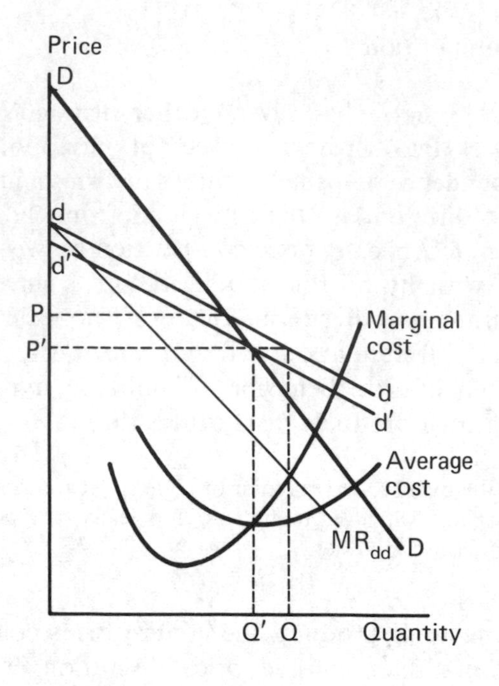

Figure 6-1a. Monopolistic Competition in the Short Run Quantity

under the *correct* assumption that their price changes will have an imperceptible effect on industry sales. They therefore operate at price level *P*′, where marginal cost equals the marginal revenue associcated with the *dd* curve. Because *all* firms adopt this rational behavior, output falls to *Q*′, the quantity associated with price *P*′ on the actual demand curve. Firms then equate marginal cost with the marginal revenue associated with the newly established perceived demand curve *d′d′*. This procedure continues until the perceived marginal revenue curve intercepts the marginal cost curve where *dd* and *DD* intercept. The so-called "short run" equilibrium is not sustainable, however, if the price where *dd* and *DD* meet is above or below the level of average cost. In this case economic profit or loss would prevail. The resulting entry or exit of firms yields the well known tangency equilibrium solution (Figure 6-1b) in the long run. Because equilibrium price equals average cost, long run profits are zero. Since the final perceived demand is tangent to the average cost

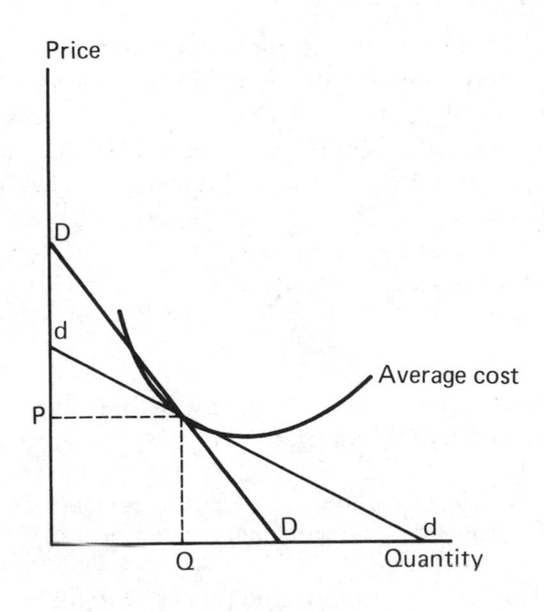

Figure 6-1b. Monopolistic Competition Long Run Equilibrium

curve, no other level of output would appear to be preferable to any firm. Thus, despite the fact that firms enjoy price discretion in the monopolistic short run, subsequent competition through firm entry yields a stable group equilibrium with competitive returns. This is the Chamberlinian result.

Some distinctions exist between the theory as offered by Professor Chamberlin and Mrs. Robinson. Readers of *The Economics of Imperfect Competition* note immediately that Mrs. Robinson's topic is broader than the theory of the firm. Perhaps revealing her Marxian antecedents, the Cambridge economist addresses subjects like the distribution of income and exploitation of labor. While Mrs. Robinson has insisted[10] that her treatment of firm behavior approximates what has become identified with Chamberlin's name, definite differences in approach exist. Probably the most notable difference is that her original formulation of imperfect competition deals with totally homogeneous goods while Chamberlin's relies crucially upon product heterogeneity. Also, imperfect competition is presented in a fundamentally competitive rather than monopolistic framework. Other differences have been documented by Chamberlin in no fewer than seven works.[11] In his important comparison of Robinson, Chamberlin, von Stackelberg, and Pareto, Triffin concludes that while their approaches differ substantially, Robinson and Chamberlin treat the same problem and reach similar conclusions.[12] The nature of the problem in Mrs. Robinson's view is indicated by her examples of market imperfections:

> costs of transport, location, . . . guarantee of quality provided by a well-known name, . . . differences between the facilities provided by different producers, . . . advertisement.[13]

These bear a close resemblance to many of the sources of product differentiation cited by Chamberlin:

> convenience of the seller's location, . . . exclusive patented features, . . . (the seller's) way of doing business, his reputation, . . . trademarks.[14]

The theories also have in common the tangency equilibrium solution. In this light it is easy to see why a single cohesive theory has survived from the original formulations of imperfect competition and monopolistic competition. Through nonprice competition among large numbers of firms, that theory specifies that competitive returns will prevail despite individual firm price discretion.

The theory of nonprice competition has had a profound influence on the subsequent development of microeconomic theory and industrial organization. Within less than a decade the books of Chamberlin and Robinson sparked the classic contributions of Hitch and Hall, Sweezy, and J.M. Clark.[15] A number of later articles contrasted the comparative statics, welfare implications, and equilibrium conditions of the monopolistic competition and competitive models.[16] Chamberlin's idea that industry is composed of a number of competing monopolists caused a theoretical examination of the traditional definition of markets and industries.[17] This has raised empirical issues in the literature of banking, marketing, and agricultural economics.[18] The concept of nonprice competition through product differentiation was translated into detailed consideration of one means of differentiation, advertising. In the theoretical realm Baumol, Williamson, and Horowitz have deduced the effects of advertising in sales maximation, discretionary profit, and uncertainty models of firm behavior, respectively.[19] Jostram and Heflebower have suggested theoretical means of accounting for firm investment in advertising capital.[20] On the empirical front Comanor and Wilson, Shepherd, and Telser have assessed the aggregate effect of advertising on profitability looking across industries.[21] Narrower studies[22] of food and cigarette retailing have also examined the impact of advertising within particular industries. Unfortunately, other means of nonprice competition have received considerably less attention. Apparently in only one industry, airline passenger travel, has the impact of competition in customer service and product quality been studied in detail.[23] Nevertheless, the greatest tribute to Chamberlin may be that after forty years of examination and evaluation, his resilient theory remains substantially intact.

A Model of the Brokerage Industry

In an important sense the brokerage industry represents a hybrid of oligopoly and monopolistic competition. On the one hand firms fully acknowledge their interdependence and explicitly collude with respect to price. However, industry participants have been less than successful in supplanting nonprice competition. In particular, no industry agreement establishes the levels of customer service that firms may adopt. Indeed, customer service rivalry has been regarded an "approved" form of competition within the industry.[24] Accordingly, all brokerage houses have engaged in extensive nonprice competition. As with universal price cutting in the monopolistic competition model, this widespread source of competition between firms can be expected to reduce profit. Thus, the industry presents the economic theorist with the anomaly that firms having the sophistication to fix one competitive variable are competing with respect to others.

Several factors contribute to this paradox. First, firms could act under the illusion that it is to their individual advantage to compete through nonprice means. A firm may feel that it has a product which, due to the firm's rapport with clients, its research team, or its overall understanding of the stock market, cannot be duplicated by other competitors. Such a firm would therefore raise levels of customer service believing that other firms could not successfully compete with it through nonprice means. A second reason for price oligopolists to engage in nonprice competition is possible: unlike price competition, it is very difficult to detect nonprice competition.

As has been established, brokerage firms already provide their customers with a wide range of services. A firm could covertly augment these services by improving their quality or making them available to more customers without other competitors becoming aware. Secure in the knowledge that other firms could not recognize and, thus, follow such a competitive move, firms that felt it to be in their interests to collude on price might compete through services to increase their share of the monopolistic profit. These two explanations for the extensive nonprice competition found in the brokerage industry have a common thread: in each, firms assume that their competitors will not match their increases in nonprice competition either because the other firms cannot successfully compete through services or because they cannot detect changes in levels of customer service. A third type of behavior may also explain competitive practices in the industry: like participants in a price competitive market, a company may assume that other brokerage houses will engage in competition and, due to an inability of firms to collude on levels of service, the firm itself may be forced to compete in order to protect its position. Several factors make it more difficult to collude on nonprice variables than to fix price. First, while the SEC has fostered commission fixing, it believes, as has been discussed, that service competition is beneficial. It is not clear that the Commission would countenance any attempt to limit service competition. One must remember, too, that for 180 years NYSE member firms have possessed a means of proposing, ratifying, and enforcing minimum price agreements. The absence of corresponding institutions for colluding on nonprice competition makes it more difficult for firms to collude on levels of service. Most important, however, is the fact that, whereas price is a homogeneous competitive variable, nonprice competition is multifaceted. In order to fix levels of service all sources of service competition would have to be quantified as well as identified. Not only would the number of research advisories provided to customers have to be fixed, but their length, form, medium, and quality would have to be limited. In the same way, supplanting service competition would require placing limits on the number, training, and experience of registered representatives as well as on the location, appearance, and number of brokerage offices. The imagination that brokerage firms have displayed in developing new means of nonprice competition would further complicate the administration of such a collusive agreement. For these reasons, brokerage firms as a practical matter may be unable to supplant nonprice competition. Aware that at least some of the 500 firms in the industry may raise levels of service to attract customers from noncompeting firms, all brokerage houses are forced to compete.[25] They act like oligopolists in setting price and like competitors in establishing levels of customer service.

Deriving the implications of this hypothesis requires a unique theoretical tool. Conventional oligopoly models have little to say about nonprice competition. By the same token, it is clear from Figure 6-1 that long run equilibrium in the monopolistic competition model relies on freedom of entry and price competition, forces which are absent in the brokerage industry. However, the traditional presentation of Chamberlin's theory also holds levels of nonprice competition fixed. When, instead, firms are allowed to vary their levels of customer service, such nonprice competition reduces profit irrespective of entry and pricing practices. That proposition, recognized by Stigler and Horowitz,[26] depends upon the costs of nonprice competition, a central feature of monopolistic competition as it was originally formulated by Chamberlin.[27] An adaptation of Chamberlin's original model will be used to analyze nonprice competition within the brokerage industry. Throughout the analysis it will be assumed that brokerage firms are of equal size with similar cost structures. The existence of standard measures of output and price is also postulated.

In setting price, each brokerage firm is said to face demand curve $D(N^f, N^o)$ in Figure 6-2a, representing its share of industry demand. For well known reasons, profit would be maximized at output V^1 where marginal cost of production is equal to marginal revenue. Because collusive pricing and barriers to entry enjoy legal sanction in the industry, members of the Exchange are able to coordinate their commission rates. Acting in the manner of oligopolists, firms therefore adopt the profit maximizing rate C^*.

If an entrepreneur were certain that he would not be followed by other entrepreneurs, he would have an incentive to undercut the commission rate that maximizes collective profits in order to increase demand by attracting business from rival brokers. Widespread adoption of this course of action would reduce commission rates to competitive levels. The threat of such *sub rosa* price competition is recognized as the major problem in cartel management.[28] In this industry, however, Securities and Exchange Commission sanction of

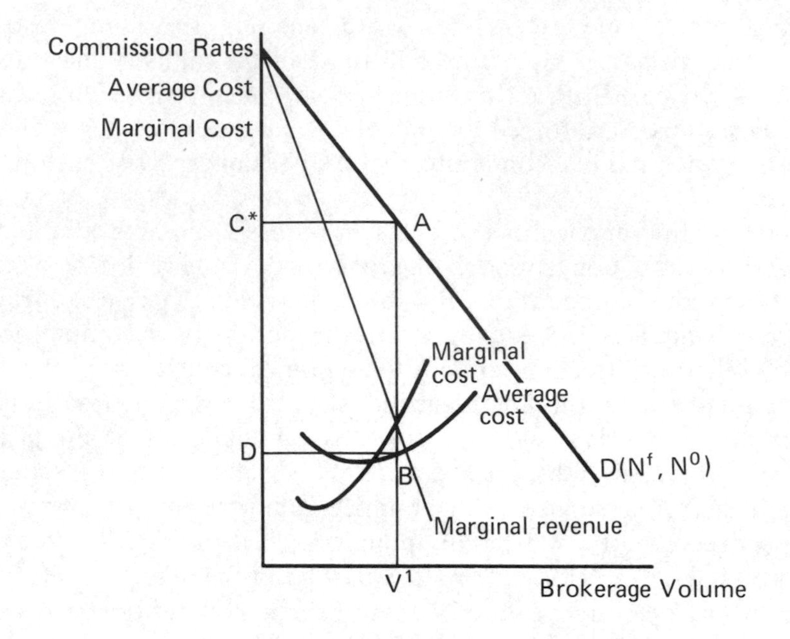

Figure 6-2a. Oligopolistic Pricing in the Brokerage Industry I

price fixing removes that threat. Colluding firms acting through the NYSE can legally expel from the central marketplace firms which shade commission rates. Thus, only one round of commission cutting has occurred in NYSE history. As was discussed in Chapter 3, this price competition took place in 1929, the industry's most profitable year. In general, though, all brokerage houses charge the cooperatively established minimum rate *C**. All receive the associated level of profit, *CABD*. This is analogous to Chamberlin's monopolistic short run equilibrium solution.

The collusive behavior that characterizes rate setting within the industry does not extend to service competition. As mentioned above, several factors may explain the propensity of brokerage houses to engage in extensive nonprice competition: a conviction among firms that their customer services cannot be duplicated; the difficulty of detecting nonprice competition by other firms; and the inability of the industry to collude in setting levels of customer service. Just as the firm has an incentive to lower its commission rates secretly, companies are motivated to increase customer services in order to expand demand. However, for firms to engage in nonprice competition it is not sufficient that they merely perceive that increased services will raise the amount of brokerage demanded by customers. Beyond this, it must be anticipated that the increase in revenues associated with such nonprice competition more than offsets the associated increase in costs. Only this conviction can explain the universal participation in customer service competition by member firms of the New York Stock Exchange.

The analytics of nonprice competition rely on the two shift parameters of the demand curve facing brokerage houses: N^f, the firm's level of customer services, and N^O, the level of customer services offered by other firms. D is assumed to shift to the right with increasing N^f and to the left with increases in N^O. This of course reflects the assumption that a firm's share of industry demand will rise when it offers more customer services or fall when other firms provide additional services. In the model of the brokerage industry, C is established on the basis of the prevailing values of N^f and N^O which determine $D(N^f, N^O)$. However, after C is agreed upon a higher level of N^f may shift demand by more than enough to offset the attendant increase in cost. For example (Figure 6-2b), associated with the level of services $N^{f'}$ are the demand curve $D(N^{f'}, N^O)$ and the short run average cost curve $AC(V, N^{f'})$, which includes the costs of both output V and the prevailing level of nonprice competition $N^{f'}$. As is indicated by the lower part of the figure, a shift to level of services $N^{f'}$ would, holding other things the same, raise firm profit from P^1 to P^2.

It is hypothesized that firms act under the illusion that changes in their levels of customer service will not be followed by other firms. In the brokerage industry, this Chamberlinian assumption has reasonable basis. As has been discussed, entrepreneurs may believe that, due to the nature of customer services, their competitive moves either cannot be duplicated or cannot be detected by competitors. Acting under this illusion, firms will offer the level of services $N^{f'}$ with the expectation of earning profit P^2. However, other firms have similar motivations and adopt the same course of action, shifting the perceived demand curve back to the left. The effects of N^f and N^O are therefore offsetting.[29] Like price competition in the monopolistic competition model, nonprice competition is self-defeating.

Note that it is not necessary to assume that *all* firms act under

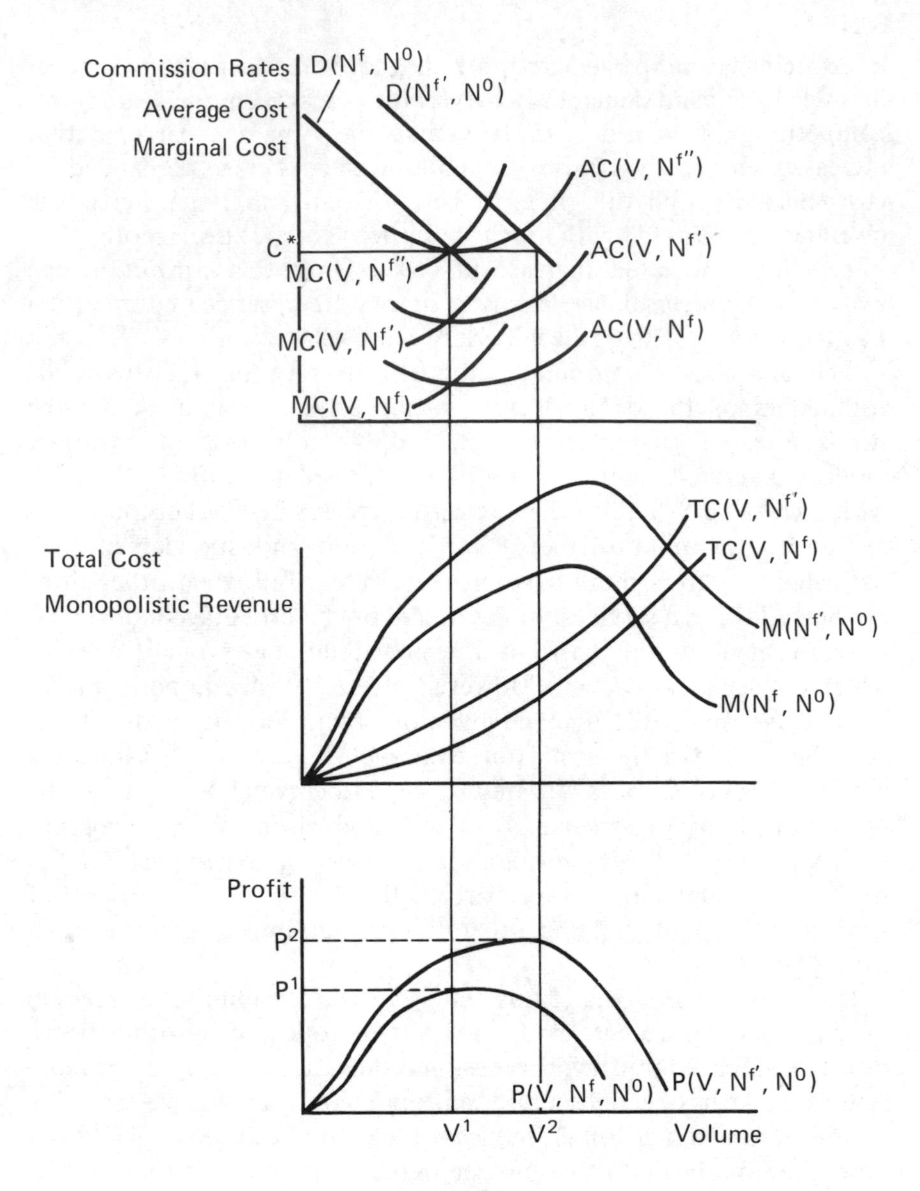

Figure 6-2b. Oligopolistic Pricing in the Brokerage Industry II

illusion. Assume, instead, that a firm initially refrains from competing through services in recognition of the potential impact on profit. Even if only a small portion of the 500 industry participants engages in nonprice competition, the refraining firm will notice diminished demand. That is, because the level of services (N^O) offered by the firm's competitors increases, the refraining firm's demand curve will shift to the left. With price fixed and collusion on levels of service impossible, the firm will itself have to raise levels of customer service to regain and maintain its market position. Given the difficulty of ascertaining competitors' exact levels of service, the firm may adopt a level of service higher than $N^{f'}$, leading to a further increase by other firms. Thus, just as a price cutter acting in a market where price is not colluded upon can cause a price war, so the decision by a small number of firms to increase levels of service could lead to a "service war." The rivalry in services described in Chapter 5 suggests that this analogy may be particularly apt.

Continuing customer service competition has the obvious effect of raising costs to the firm. Higher selling costs are reflected in the average short run cost curves shown in Figure 6-2b. These costs place a limit on the extent of nonprice competition. Because firms would prefer to risk losing market share to operating at a loss continually, they will not raise service above the level $N^{f''}$ where average cost equals average revenue. At this point, however, the oligopoly profit associated with price fixing in Figure 6-2a, *CABD*, has been eliminated through nonprice competition.

In the interpretation of the brokerage industry presented in this chapter, oligopolistic power in the short run leads to economic profit. Federally sanctioned policies restrict subsequent price competition and entry. However, customer service competition, which is not subject to collusive control, brings about a firm and group equilibrium in which profit is diminished. In place of entry and price, the model endows firms with a host of variables–the levels of various types of customer services–with which to make competitive responses. Even if a firm realizes that nonprice competition will eventually reduce profits, it must increase these services in order to remain competitive itself. It is therefore hypothesized that nonprice competition in the brokerage industry exerts the pressures normally associated with price competition and free entry.[30]

The temporal implications of the model of nonprice competition and noncompetitive pricing are summarized in Figure 6-3 under the *ceteris paribus* assumption. As the model illustrates, the ability of brokerage firms to collude on price maximizes industry profit. Firms react to this profit by offering additional customer services to raise their share of earnings. This nonprice competition continues in successive periods as the firms, unable to fix levels of service, try to

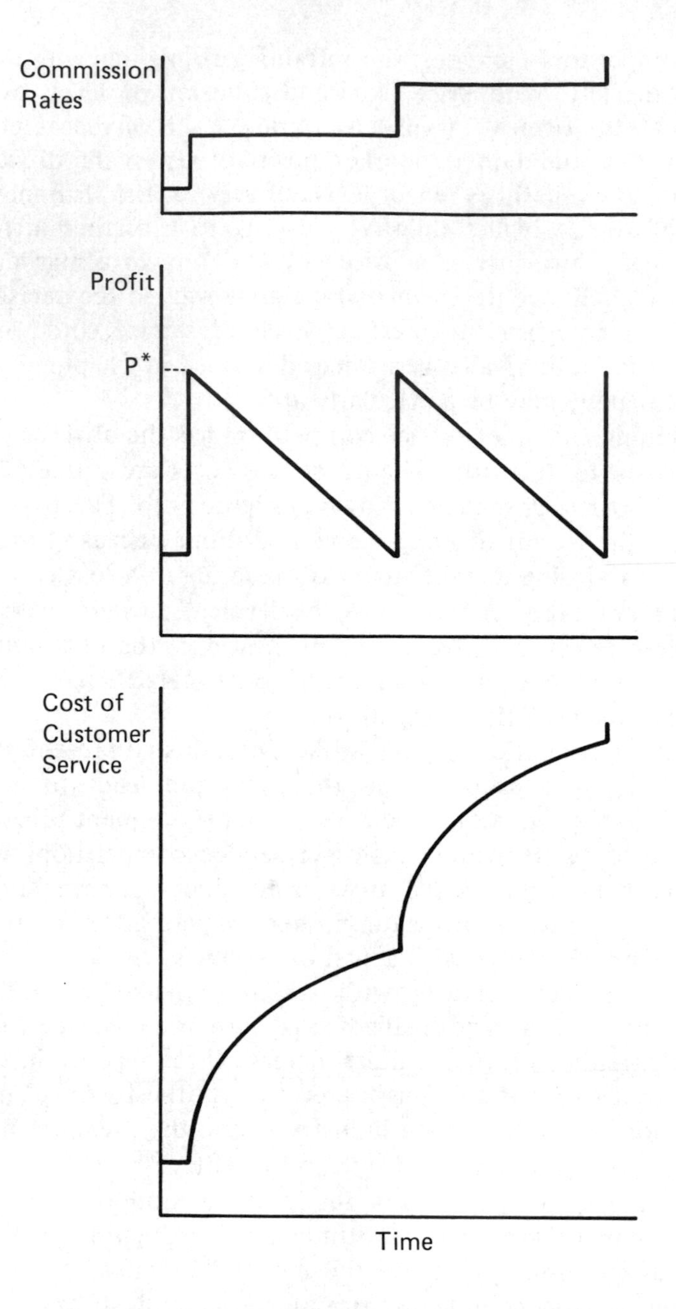

Figure 6-3. Competitive Variables over Time

protect their market positions (Figure 6-3). Because all firms eventually compete, the effect of service competition is to reduce broker profits from their initial levels. The oligopolistic profit of NYSE member firms cannot be sustained because all competitive variables are not subject to collusive control.

Conclusions

It is hypothesized that brokerage firms act oligopolistically in setting price and competitively in establishing levels of customer service. The paradox that firms recognize their interdependence yet compete has three sources: individual firms may feel that they have a comparative advantage in service competition; because changing levels of customer service cannot be detected, firms may believe that their nonprice competition will not be noticed and, therefore, not followed; and, finally, since it is very difficult collusively to fix levels of service, firms that suspect others in the large industry of attempting to increase their market share through nonprice competition will themselves be forced to compete in order to protect their own market positions. For these reasons, extensive nonprice competition is witnessed in the shadow of strictly enforced price collusion.

A model that employs Chamberlin's selling costs analysis under conditions of price fixing and restricted entry provides these theoretical predictions:

1. Federally sanctioned New York Stock Exchange policies fixing commission rates and limiting market entry in the first instance increase profits in the brokerage industry.
2. With other sources of competition restricted, extensive nonprice competition through customer services arises in response to those profits.
3. This nonprice competition diminishes the returns associated with collusion among NYSE member firms.

These propositions prevail when other influences are held constant.

7 The Empirical Evidence

Instead of drawing its substance from arbitrary assumptions, chosen for their simplicity and unduly extended to the whole field of economic activity, our theory may turn to more pedestrian, but more fruitful methods. It will recognize the richness and variety of all concrete cases, and tackle each problem with due respect for its individual aspects. More advantage will be taken of all relevant factual information, and less reliance will be placed on a mere resort to the passkey of general theoretical assumptions.

– Robert Triffin

Empirical analysis at the industry level can verify whether or not the behavior of brokerage firms approximates that represented in the model of Chapter 6. In particular, the validity of the three theoretical predictions can be evaluated on a historical basis. Econometric techniques also provide quantitative estimates of the influence of the determinants of conduct within the brokerage industry. The final goal of this empirical analysis is an estimate of the relative significance of noncompetitive pricing and nonprice competition to industry performance.

The Model

The theoretical relationships between commissions, profit, and customer service competition depicted in Figure 6-3 are said to hold when other influences remain unchanged. Clearly the *ceteris paribus* assumption is not applicable when empirical evidence is considered. In particular, the impact of changing demand must be accounted for in explaining levels of industry commissions, profit, and nonprice competition. To this end, Figure 7-1 is introduced.

The monopolistic revenue curve $M(V)$ in Figure 7-1 indicates the revenue received by each firm for any level of brokerage volume V.

Robert Triffin, *Monopolistic Competition and General Equilibrium Theory*, p. 189.

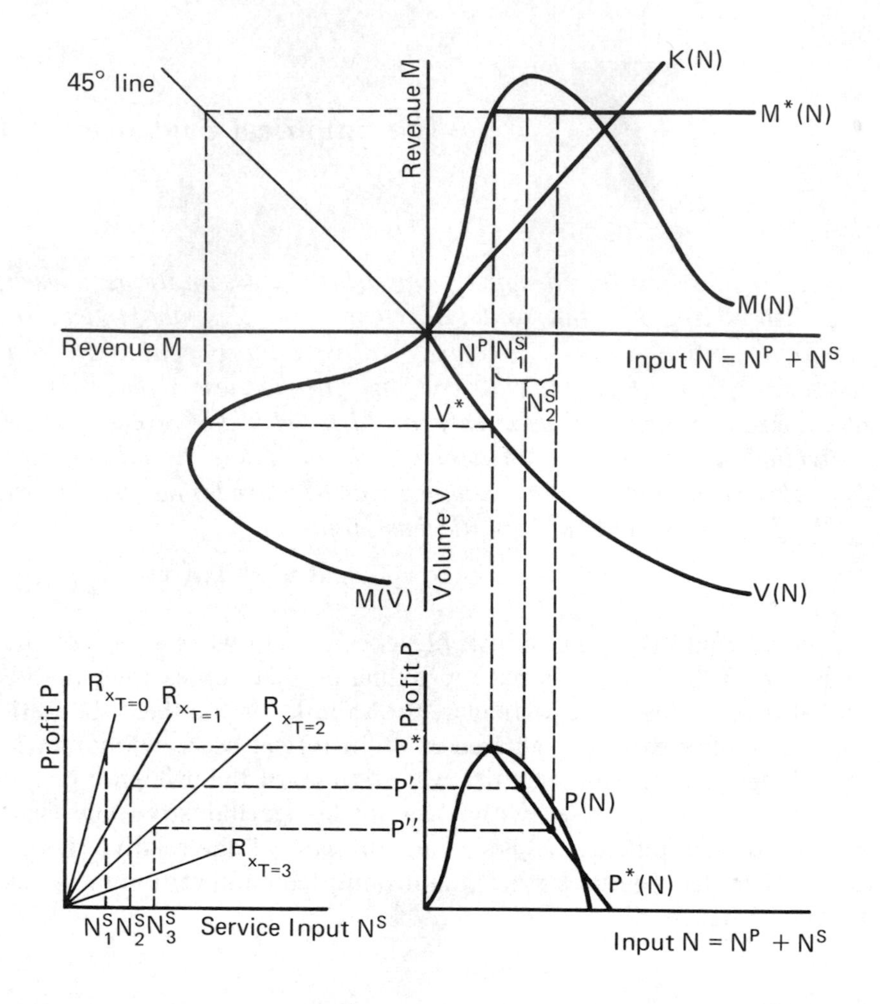

Figure 7-1. A Model of the Brokerage Industry

Associated with each point on $M(V)$ is some commission rate C. Using the production function $V(N)$ and the 45-degree line, $M(V)$ is mapped into revenue-input space in quadrant I. The cost function $K(N)$ is linear under the assumption of constant factor prices. Profit, $P(N)$, is readily derived from $M(N)$ and $K(N)$ in Figure 7-1. Because brokerage firms are able to collude, they operate at the profit maximizing level of output V^* produced by input N^P. They will adopt and enforce the corresponding commission rate C^*.

Firms are assumed to seek a greater part of the oligopolistic profit by engaging in nonprice competition. That is, they desire to shift to a higher revenue function by augmenting levels of customer service. To produce more services, factors of production will be employed in addition to N^P, the input necessary to produce brokerage volume V*. However, with all firms engaging in nonprice competition, revenue does not change as inputs to customer service increase. Thus, once C* is adopted, the horizontal revenue function M*(N) is defined for levels of input greater than N^P. M*(N) determines the profit function P*(N). Like the DD curve in the Chamberlinian large numbers case, M*(N) and P*(N) obtain because all firms engage in competition.

It is postulated that the greater the collusive profit, the more input the firm will be willing to devote to improving customer services in order to shift its revenue curve. In addition, nonprice competition is said to increase over time as all firms augment their levels of service to protect their market positions. These responses are embodied in the reaction curves shown in Figure 7-1. In the first period after adoption of commission rate C* ($T = 0$), firms react to profit P* by adding input in the amount N_1^S, however, costs rise. Because revenue is fixed at M*(N), profit falls to P'. As nonprice competition continues in successive periods, the reaction curves trace out the time path of profit along P*(N).

Several functional dependencies are indicated by this analysis. First, profit varies positively with the level of commission rates since raising brokerage fees to C* increases P. The slope of P*(N) in Figure 7-1 reveals that P is an inverse function of N. The reaction functions suggest that levels of factor employment rise in response to increased profit. In addition, N is a direct function of the shift parameter T, the number of years since a commission change (Figure 7-1). Because the observed input levels include factors that are employed to produce brokerage as well as those that produce services, the level of input N is also influenced by V. Thus, if firms collude on price and compete on service, P will vary directly with C and inversely with N, while N will move directly with P, V, and T for a given level of demand.

As has been noted, demand in the brokerage industry is subject to considerable variation. Shifts in the demand curve facing NYSE brokers arise from two sources: changes in DV, the value of all stock transactions, and change in R, the proportion of transactions which occur on other exchanges. The effect of these variables is introduced into the model through the revenue functions. For example an increase in DV or a decrease in R represents a rise in the demand for NYSE brokerage services. This shifting demand would raise revenue at every level of V and N. Within the model it is clear that increasing revenue augments profit. As a result, profit can be said to vary directly with DV and inversely with R. Shifting demand affects levels of factor employment through P, which has already been proposed as an argument of N.

This analysis suggests that the following relationships will hold:

$$N_i = f(P, V, T) \qquad (1) \text{ to } (m)$$

$$P = f(C, N_1, N_2, \ldots N_m, DV, R) \qquad (m + 1)$$

where the variables are defined as follows:

- P – a proxy for NYSE member firm profitability.
- N_i – levels of service-rendering factors of production.
- C – a measure of commission rates.
- DV – volume of all U.S. transactions in dollars.
- R – regional stock exchange volume of transactions in dollars.
- T – the number of years since a commission rate adjustment.
- V – volume of transactions on the NYSE in number of shares.

The theory developed above predicts that the coefficients of all variables except R and the N_i terms in Equation $(m + 1)$ will be positive. The empirical analysis which follows has as its goal verification of these functional dependencies.

As was discussed in Chapter 2, the price of NYSE seats, adjusted for the increased number of seats in 1929, capitalizes the profit associated with Exchange membership. Because the Exchange has published industry earnings only since 1966, the adjusted value of memberships is adopted as a proxy for profit in the variable P. C is the commission rate variable employed in Chapter 3. It represents the commission rate on a round lot trade of a \$50.00 stock. Three variables are used to measure the quality of customer service:

N_b – the number of stock brokers per firm.
N_e – the number of nonbroker employees per firm.
N_o – the number of offices per firm.

These definitions are used since factor cost data are not available for years prior to 1966.[1] Variables P, C, DV, and R are expressed in constant dollars.

The econometric test consists of $m + 1$ equations in $m + 6$ variables. The price of NYSE memberships, a proxy for industry profitability, is determined within the model as are three sources of service competition. Commission rates, the timing of commission rate changes, NYSE volume in number and value of shares traded, and regional stock exchange volume are regarded as exogenously determined influences.

Econometric Considerations

Preliminary estimations of the system of Equations (1) to (m + 1) for the period 1955 to 1972 involved only contemporaneous terms for each variable. Because profitability both influences and is influenced by levels of customer service, the model embodied an obvious simultaneity. To incorporate the simultaneous nature of this specification of the model, the two-stage least squares method of estimation was originally adopted.[2] However, when the sample period was expanded to include pre-1955 observations, lagged values of P in Equations (1) to (m) proved to be superior predictors of nonprice competition judging from the percentage of explained variance and the standard error of the estimated coefficient of the profit variable. Experimentation with the Almon technique[3] for estimating polynomial distributed lags indicated that only the previous year's value of P significantly influences levels of nonprice competition. Hence, a single lagged term, P_{t-1}, was included in Equations (1) to (m). Replacing contemporaneous values of P with a lagged value makes the system of equations recursive rather than simultaneous because levels of nonprice competition in any period influence the current level of profitability but not vice versa.[4] The system of equations can therefore be estimated employing the ordinary least squares method.

The error terms of the estimated equations exhibited substantial serial correlation as measured by the Durbin-Watson statistic. To remedy this condition, the Cochrane-Orcutt[5] technique was employed in all estimations. This widely used procedure estimates the coefficient of correlation and uses it to transform the data in an iterative process. The revised Durbin-Watson statistics indicate that the procedure successfully removed the autocorrelation found in estimations of the untransformed data. Unlike the original least squares estimations, the reported coefficient estimates are regarded as efficient and the associated t, R^2, and F statistics are accepted as valid.

Data for the variables N_b, N_e, and N_o were available for different periods of time.[6] In order to use all the data, three equations for profit were estimated separately, one for each of the customer service terms. A single estimation of Equation m using the three N_i arguments could have been made only for the period in which data for all variables were available. This would have limited the degrees of freedom of all the equations.

Empirical Results

The estimated equations[7] are reported in Table 7-1. In general, the relationships are strong. Each equation explains a large percentage of

Table 7-1
Estimated Equations

	R^2	F	$D\text{-}W^*$
1. $N_b = 0.0179\,P_{t-1} + 0.0235\,V + 0.174\,T + 189.5$ (0.0085) (0.0171) (0.105) (69.8)	0.99	1821.0	2.38
2. $N_e = 0.154\,P_{t-1} + 0.448\,V + 0.623\,T + 52.68$ (0.024) (0.022) (0.400) (4.08)	0.99	1054.1	2.19
3. $N_o = 0.00125\,P_{t-1} + 0.00406\,V + 0.00384\,T + 6.89$ (0.00062) (0.00123) (0.00808) (1.68)	0.99	1245.2	1.89
4a. $P = -3.67\,N_b + 2.56\,C - 13.85\,R + 5.10\,DV - 70.45$ (1.00) (1.41) (4.50) (0.66) (85.15)	0.95	111.9	1.93
4b. $P = -1.17\,N_e + 3.56\,C - 17.18\,R + 5.36\,DV - 117.5$ (0.60) (2.38) (5.86) (0.94) (142.9)	0.92	51.1	1.85
4c. $P = -44.4\,N_o + 3.76\,C - 12.30\,R + 4.59\,DV - 72.62$ (24.98) (1.74) (5.51) (0.89) (5.15)	0.92	77.3	1.79

Parenthetical figures represent standard errors.
*Durbin-Watson Statistic

the variance of the dependent term. In the case of the reaction equations, virtually all of the variance is accounted for. Only the coefficient of T in Equation 3 is not significantly different from zero at the 90% level.[8] The F statistics indicate that each of the linear relationships is significant as a whole at the 1% level. At the same level of confidence, the hypotheses of positive and negative autocorrelation can be rejected for all equations as estimated.

The shift parameters of Equations 1 through 4c carry the expected signs. Regardless of competitive conditions, the levels of productive factors per member firm increase with the physical volume of NYSE transactions (Equations 1, 2, and 3). The positive coefficients on DV in Equations 4a, 4b, and 4c indicate that higher levels of dollar volume raise profits, other things being the same. Finally, the value of regional stock exchange transactions appears as a negative influence on profitability. This verifies that trading on regional exchanges is a substitute for NYSE brokerage.

The empirical results of Table 7-1 substantiate the theoretical specifications of the last chapter. The significantly positive coefficients on C in Equations 4a, 4b, and 4c, indicate that higher commission rates increase profitability within the brokerage industry. The coefficients of P_{t-1} in Equations 1 to 3 verify that greater profit in one period leads to increased levels of customer service in the succeeding period. Finally, the negative impact of increased nonprice competition is captured by the coefficients of the N_b, N_e, and N_o variables in the profitability equations. Each of these relationships shows a high degree of statistical significance. The weakest, the effect of commission rates on profitability, is valid at the 92% level or higher. The positive coefficients on T in the equations for N_b and N_e also indicate that brokerage houses systematically raise the number of broker and nonbroker employees in years following commission rates changes, abstracting from differences in the volume of transactions. These results collectively validate the hypothesis that nonprice competition reduces the profitability associated with price fixing in the brokerage industry.

The quantitative effects of the determinants of profitability and nonprice competition are estimated in an absolute sense by the coefficients in Table 7-1. The relative importance of these determinants, however, is most accurately assessed with reference to their proportional effects. To this end the partial elasticities of the arguments of Equations 1, 2, and 3, evaluated at mean values of the variables, are reported in Table 7-2. The proportional influence of the determinants of profitability are shown in Table 7-3.

Levels of N_b, N_e, and N_o appear to be inelastic with respect to changes in volume of stock exchange transactions. A ten percent increment in volume is at the margin associated with a 4.4% change in the number of nonbroker employees hired by NYSE firms. The same increment leads to 1.13% and 0.69% variations in N_o and N_b, respectively. The low responsiveness of these variables suggests that firms enjoy substantial efficiencies in employing brokers, offices, and nonbroker employees to produce stock brokerage. A one percent increase in the number of brokers, for example, can accommodate 14% growth in volume of transactions. While as was seen in Chapter 3 small firms control exchange policies, there appear to be unexploited economies associated with large scale production.

Elasticity calculations reveal that the number of nonbroker employees hired per firm is the nonprice competition variable most sensitive to changes in P_{t-1} and T. N_e varies from 2.5 to 4.0 times more to changes in profitability than do N_b and N_o. Several sources may contribute to the propensity of brokerage firms to favor changes in back office customer services in responding to competitive conditions. First, firms may find that these services are more effective in attracting and retaining customers. In addition, varying levels of registered representative services, as an alternative, might at times require dismissing stock brokers. Due to the strong broker-client relationship that frequently exists, a firm which fired a broker in hard times might lose his accounts. As was discussed in Chapter 1, brokerage back office personnel are not highly trained, while brokers receive as much as $15,000 in formal preparation. For this reason,

Table 7-2
Partial Elasticities of Nonprice Competition Variables

		$\frac{\partial N_i}{\partial X} \Big/ \frac{\overline{N_i}}{\overline{X}}$		
X	$\overline{X}$	$N_i = N_b$	$N_i = N_e$	$N_i = N_o$
P_{t-1}	154.4	0.069	0.180	0.046
V	115.1	0.069	0.443	0.113
T	4.1	0.018	0.020	0.000

Table 7-3
Partial Elasticities of Profit (*P*)

		$\frac{\partial P}{\partial X} \Big/ \frac{\bar{P}}{\bar{X}}$		
			Equation	
X	$\bar{X}$	4a	4b	4c
N_b	39.1	−0.930		
N_e	109.0		−0.972	
N_o	4.1			−1.186
C	52.2	0.865	1.005	1.270
R	5.5	−0.497	−0.681	−0.441
DV	61.2	2.020	2.301	1.962

brokerage houses would be more willing to vary levels of nonbroker employment when conditions warrant.[9] Another form of competitive response, opening branch offices, has even greater fixed costs. Increasing overhead costs is patently undesirable in an industry characterized by widely varying levels of demand. Thus, the number of nonbroker employees in the industry is the customer service variable most responsive to changes in profit and timing of commission rate changes. The number of offices per firm is least responsive.

The elasticities of profit with respect to changes in N_b and N_e are of the same order of magnitude. A 10% rise in the number of brokers or nonbroker employees is estimated to lower profit by 9.3 and 9.7 percent, respectively (Table 7-3). A similar increase in the number of branch offices would reduce profitability by 11.9%, though. The greater impact of this mode of competition is consistent with its relatively low responsiveness to changes in P_{t-1} (Table 7-2). Aware that opening new offices has potentially greater adverse impact on earnings, brokerage houses appear to favor other types of competitive response.

Nonprice Competition versus Noncompetitive Pricing

In order to assess the relative impact of price fixing and nonprice competition in the industry, simulated time paths of P, N_b, N_o, and

N_e can be generated from the estimated equations. The mean values of the variables during the 1942-1972 sample period are used as initial values. During that period commission rates rose an average of once every 7.5 years. The mean increase was 27.9%. Figures 7-2, 7-3, and 7-4 represent the time paths of the profit and nonprice competition variables assuming that as an initial shock, C is raised by 27.9%. The data[10] on which the figures are based are shown in Table 7-4. The percentage change in P is also shown.

The calculated time paths are of the same general form as the theoretical ones derived in the last chapter (Figure 6-3). The initial effect of higher commission rates is to increase profitability. This induces brokers to raise levels of customer service, reducing profit in subsequent periods. The derived time paths of the proxy for profit illustrate the adverse impact of each measure of nonprice competition. The aggregate effect of these sources of competition within the industry is approximated by Figure 7-5. There, the mean peak value of P has been reduced by the sum of the percentage decrement in P associated with increasing levels of N_b, N_e, and N_o in each period.

The effect of price collusion in the brokerage industry is impressive. Depending on which equation for P is employed, a 27.9% increase in C raises the measure of profits by from 23% to 35%. However, in succeeding years nonprice competition reduces profitability from this peak. During the second year after a commission rate increase, service competition in the form of hiring additional broker and nonbroker employees reduces the initial rise in profitability by 2.0 and 6.6 percentage points respectively. The opening of new offices is estimated to lower profitability by another 2.1%. The estimated equations indicate that after seven and one-half years higher levels of N_b, N_e and N_o cause 4.0, 7.8, and 2.6 percentage point decrements in profits, respectively. The sum of these figures, 14.4%, approximates the upper limit of the total effect of these forms of competition in reducing the proxy for broker profits from its peak level. Thus, while noncompetitive pricing substantially augments the profitability of New York Stock Exchange member firms, up to one-half of the profit associated with their price collusion is consumed by competition among firms in adding registered representatives, back office employees, and new offices to improve customer service.

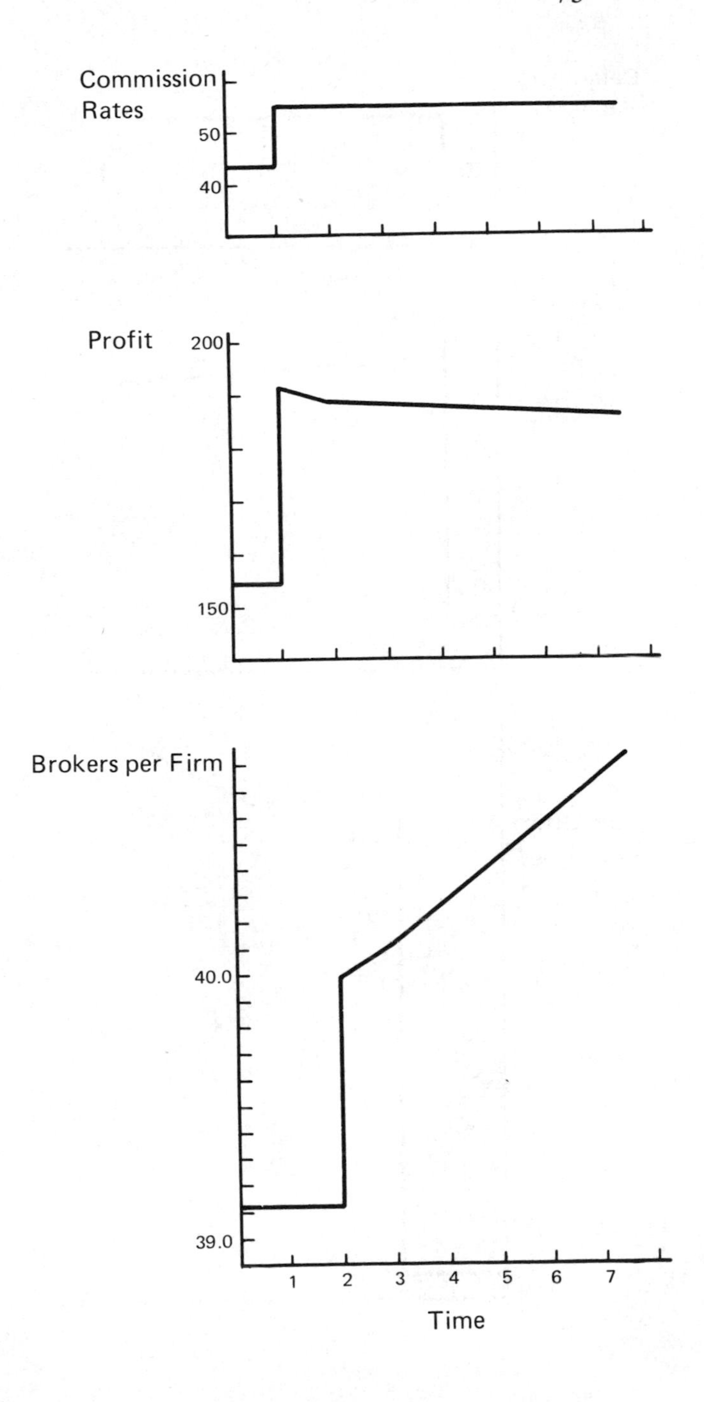

Figure 7-2. The Effect of N_b over Time

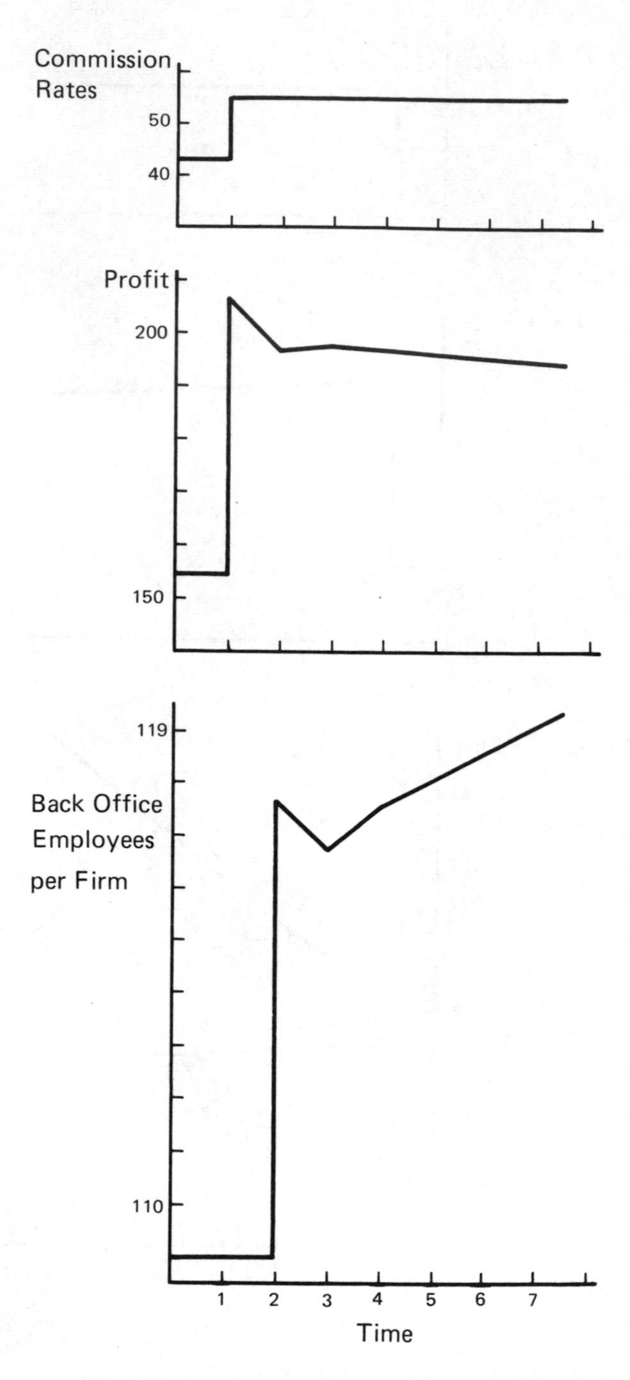

Figure 7-3. The Effect of N_e over Time

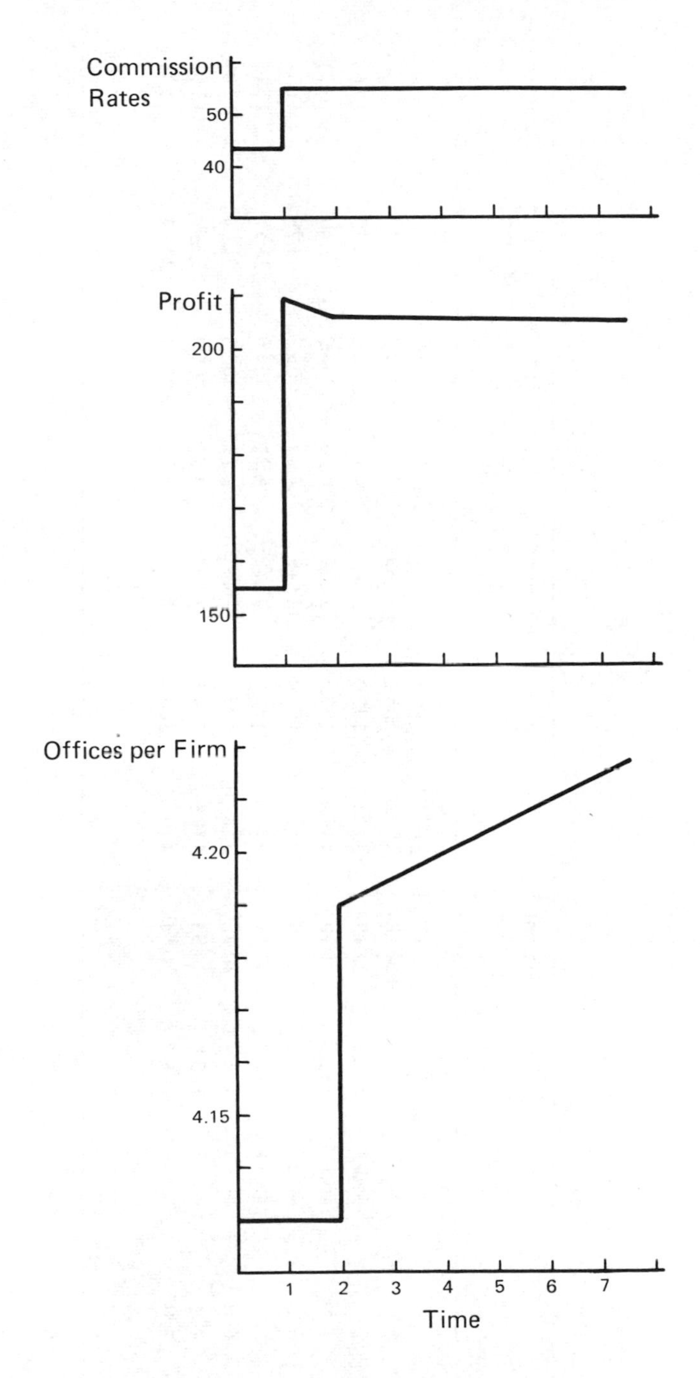

Figure 7-4. The Effect of N_O over Time

Table 7-4
Estimated Time Paths

Period	N_b	P	Percent Change in P	N_e	P	Percent Change in P	N_o	P	Percent Change in P	Total Percent Decrement from Peak P
0	39.14	154.4		109.03	154.4		4.13	154.4		
1	39.14	191.7	+24.18	109.03	206.3	+33.63	4.13	209.2	+35.48	
2	39.99	188.6	22.18	117.69	196.2	27.07	4.19	206.0	33.40	10.65
3	40.11	188.2	21.90	116.75	197.3	27.79	4.20	206.0	33.40	10.21
4	40.27	187.6	21.50	117.54	196.4	27.19	4.20	205.8	33.29	11.32
5	40.44	187.0	21.11	118.02	195.8	26.82	4.21	205.6	33.19	12.17
6	40.60	186.4	20.72	118.56	195.2	26.42	4.21	205.5	33.08	13.07
7	40.76	185.8	20.33	119.08	194.6	26.02	4.21	205.3	32.98	13.95
7.5	40.84	185.5	20.14	119.35	194.3	25.82	4.22	205.2	32.92	14.41
Decrement in P from its peak			4.04%			7.81%			2.56%	

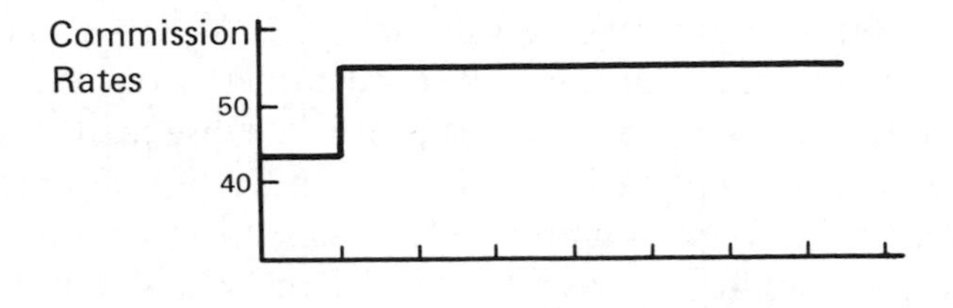

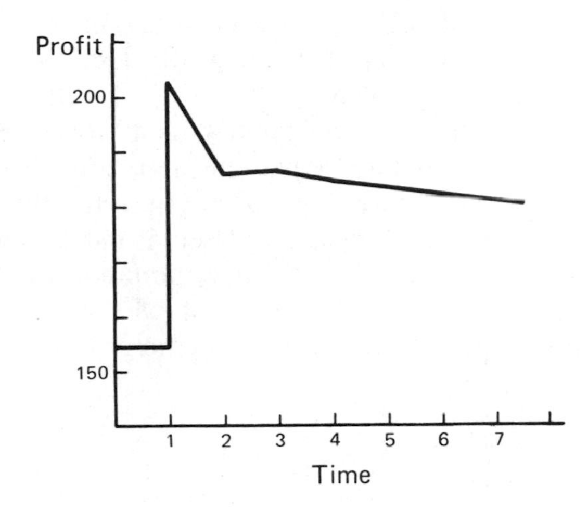

Figure 7-5. The Effect of All Sources of Nonprice Competition over Time

Conclusions

1. The multiple regression results presented in Table 7-1 are consistent with the theoretical model of the brokerage industry derived in the last chapter.

2. The number of broker and nonbroker employees and the number of offices per NYSE member firm successfully capture nonprice competitive behavior among brokerage firms. That is, in response to the greater profit associated with exercising their control over

commission rates, brokerage houses increase N_b, N_e, and N_o to attract customers through improved customer services. However, greater nonprice competition reduces profit in subsequent periods.

3. The elasticities reported in Table 7-3 indicate that competition through opening additional branch offices has the most severe impact on broker profitability. Consistent with the cost structure of the industry noted in Chapter 1, brokerage firms exhibit greater responsiveness to competitive conditions in establishing levels of back office help and, secondarily, broker employees.

4. Brokerage firms appear to enjoy substantial economies in employing additional offices, stock brokers, and, to a lesser degree, nonbroker personnel notwithstanding the fact that smaller firms control industry pricing policy.

5. The time paths of profitability and nonprice competition determined by the estimated equations approximate the theoretical paths predicted in Figure 6-3. They indicate that competition through the three means discussed offsets as much as one-half of the economic profit associated with the monopolistic pricing power brokerage houses possess. The greatest part of this reduction in profits occurs in the second year after a commission change.

8 Conclusions

The preceding seven chapters have analyzed the role of nonprice competition in the face of the noncompetitive pricing and entry policies of New York Stock Exchange member firms. The principal conclusions of the study are described below. Their public policy implications are then briefly assessed.

Summary

Brokerage houses comprise a service industry primarily engaged in buying and selling securities as agents for the public. The industry has three distinct sources of nonprice competition: registered representatives, back office staff members, and brokerage offices. These are employed jointly to provide securities brokerage and certain customer services intended to promote brokerage sales. The price at which brokerage is sold in the United States is collusively established by New York Stock Exchange member firms. Smaller, less efficient firms have defended and controlled Exchange pricing policy in the past. Despite the emergence of price competition in the Third Market, the NYSE has been able to enforce its commission structure among its members through stiff penalties. The Exchange has also acted to restrict market entry.

Its pricing and entry policies notwithstanding, a number of competitive features distinguish the brokerage industry. First, very large numbers prevail in all areas of industry activity. Brokerage firms appear to be extremely competitive in attracting factors of production. Until prohibited from doing so, they aggressively competed for institutional business through give-ups. Broker rivalry also exists in the provision of extra services to brokerage customers. In comparison with other American industries, such nonprice competition is intense within the brokerage business. Securities and Exchange Commission research and the success of experimental "cash and carry" brokerage plans suggest that the resulting level of customer services exceeds the needs of many investors.

Regulation of the brokerage industry developed in response to stock market abuses rather than to competitive conditions in the market for securities brokerage. Accordingly, the SEC has not historically interfered with industry pricing and entry policies. Rather, the Commission has fostered noncompetitive conduct of NYSE member firms by endorsing commission rate fixing, abolishing give-ups, and promulgating entry restrictions. Furthermore, nominal SEC supervision has insulated the industry from antitrust prosecution. While brokerage fees fell in relation to other prices prior to 1935, they have increased fifty percent faster than other prices since the emergence of the SEC.

Due to its distinctive competitive environment the brokerage industry has been characterized by monopoly pricing in the absence of monopoly returns. In Chapter 7 the price discretion possessed by Exchange member firms was estimated to augment their profit by from twenty-three to thirty-five percent. However, consistent with theoretical expectations, those earnings appeared to induce customer service rivalry, the form of competition approved by Exchange members and regulatory authorities. By viewing the industry's employment of productive factors, it is possible to discern statistically significant changes in the level of customer service. Abstracting from stock volume, the number of back office employees is the service-rendering factor most responsive to changing competitive conditions. The number of offices is the variable least responsive at the margin. These results are consistent with cost conditions in the industry. A *Wall Street Journal* estimate and the level of commissions in the Third Market suggest that the aggressive pursuit of customer service competition significantly raises broker costs. The econometric model cited above confirms this effect. Adding registered representatives, back office personnel, and offices to improve levels of customer service is estimated to offset as much as one-half of the profit associated with price fixing by NYSE firms. Thus, the model captures an industrial scenario in which monopolistic commission rates cause abnormal profits which lead to increased nonprice competition which in turn raises costs. Completing this dynamic relationship is the practice among member firms of basing proposals to raise commissions on the higher costs they face. These circular forces would appear to have few long term benefits for either industry participants or investors.

Policy Implications

The structure and conduct of the brokerage industry work against the public interest in three ways. NYSE pricing and entry policies protected by the SEC permit brokerage firms monopoly power in establishing commission rates. As a result of the industry's price discretion, the brokerage fees paid by investors are substantially higher on the NYSE than the competitively established Third Market rates. Furthermore, smaller firms possessing cost disadvantages have directed Exchange pricing policy. As a result, the conduct of the industry has harbored inefficiency. Finally, industry and regulatory approval of nonprice competition as the sole means of industrial rivalry has yielded a level of customer service that does not benefit many clients. In short, customers of the industry must pay monopolistically established prices for inefficiently produced securities brokerage and a level of extra services that exceeds the needs of many investors.

During the last decade, two proposals have been discussed to reorganize the sale of stock brokerage. The first provides for the "unbundling" of customer services. Under this plan services now paid for through commissions would be sold as separate products. This would tend to remedy one of the three problems cited above: clients would not be required to pay for certain services they do not desire. However, there is every reason to believe that collusively established brokerage rates and the inefficiency they protect would continue to prevail since they arise from distinctive industrial and regulatory features. Moreover, brokerage firms could be expected to compete through other nonprice means. Firms that agreed to unbundle research, account management, and back office services, for example, might very well compete through advertising and the number and appearance of their offices as long as price fixing continues. The past imagination and aggressiveness shown by brokers in initiating new services underscores a lesson to be taken from this industry: wherever price is fixed, costs will adjust to meet price.

As was mentioned in Chapter 4, the abolition of fixed commission rates has recently been proposed by regulatory authorities. This would of course be consistent with the goals of antitrust legislation applied in virtually every other industry. Prohibition of price collusion would eliminate excessive customer services as well as monopoly pricing and attendant inefficiency. This is the clear implication of the model verified above, which represents extensive service competition as arising from the economic profit associated with collusive pricing. Under competitive pricing normal returns could be expected to prevail. With lower profit and an additional means of competition, customer service rivalry would decrease. High cost firms which had been protected by fixed brokerage fees would either leave the industry or merge with other houses. In this way, abolishing fixed commission rates would eliminate the features that work contrary to the public interest in the brokerage industry.

The quantitative effects of such a policy can be deduced from the empirical results of Chapter 7. Using the Third Market as a guide, competition among NYSE members could be expected to reduce brokerage fees by from twenty to fifty-six percent. Table 7-3 indicates that a forty percent reduction in commission rates would at the margin diminish the earnings of brokers by from thirty-five to fifty-one percent. Just as the profit associated with price collusion led firms to hire additional factors capable of providing customer services, a decline in earnings could be expected to reduce levels of nonprice competition between brokers. Previously cited empirical results show that the decrease in profit associated with a forty percent reduction in commission rates would force firms to reduce their employment of registered representatives by approximately 2.4 percent; the number of nonbroker employees and offices would fall by 7.2 and 2.4 percent, respectively (Tables 7-2 and 7-3). This compares with respective declines of 3.2, 12.7, and 10.9 percent in the employment of these factors due to the 1970 drop in NYSE volume. While that year was one of the industry's worst, the comparison suggests that forbidding the Exchange to fix commission rates would have less than crippling impact. Just as eight percent of NYSE firms left the industry in the 1970 decline, freeing commission rates might cause some less efficient houses to merge or fail. Due to the very low degree of concentration present in the industry, such a contraction would not appear to threaten competition. Instead, industry efficiency would be improved. At the same time, ending price collusion by brokerage firms would break the circular relationship through which noncompetitive brokerage rates cause extensive nonprice competition and increased nonprice competition leads to still higher brokerage fees.

Appendix
Round Lot Commission Rates (1900-1974)

Period	Size of Transaction	Commission
January 1900 to May 1919	less than $1000	$ 6.25
	$1000 or more	$12.50
May 1919 to October 1924	less than $1000	$ 7.50
	$1000 - $12,499	$15.00
	$12,500 or more	$20.00
October 1924 to January 1938	less than $1000	$ 7.50
	$1000 - $2499	$12.50
	$2500 - $4999	$15.00
	$5000 - $7499	$17.50
	$7500 - $9999	$20.00
	$10,000 - $20,000	$25.00
January 1938 to March 1942	less than $100	as agreed
	$100 - $999	$5 plus $1 for each $100 over $100
	$1000 or more	$14 plus $1 for each $1000 over $1000
March 1942 to December 1947	less than $100	as agreed
	$100 - $999	$6 plus $1 for each $100 over $100
	$1000 - $8999	$15 plus 0.25% of value over $1000
	$9000 or more	$35
January 1948 to July 1953	less than $100	as agreed
	$100 - $999	$6 plus $1 for each $100 over $100
	$1000 - $3999	$15 plus $0.50 for each $100 over $1000
	$4000 - $24,999	$30 plus $1 for each $1000 over $4000
	$25,000 or more	$50

Period	Size of Transaction	Commission
July 1953 to April 1958	less than $100	as agreed
	$100 - $1999	$6 plus $1 for each $100 over $100
	$2000 - $4999	$25 plus $0.50 for each $1000 over $2000
	$5000 - $14,999	$40 plus $1 for each $100 over $5000
	$15,000 or more	$50
April 1958 to March 1972	less than $100	as agreed
	$100 - $399	$3 plus 2% (of amount traded)
	$400 - $2199	$7 plus 1%
	$2200 - $4999	$14 plus 0.5%
	$5000	$39 plus 0.1%
March 1972 to present	less than $100	as agreed
	$100 - $799	$6.40 plus 2%
	$800 - $2499	$12 plus 1.3%
	$2500 or more	$22 plus 0.9%

In March, 1972 a discount was provided for multiple round lot transactions.

Since September 25, 1973, transactions worth more than $300,000 or less than $2000 have not been subject to the NYSE commission schedule.

Sources: "Move to Increase Stock Trade Rates," *New York Times*, May 8, 1919, p. 23; "Schedule of Rates Proposed by Governors Board of NYSE," ibid, October 27, 1924, p. 35; "Exchange to Vote on Fee Increases," ibid., December 16, 1937, p. 43; "Plan to Raise Rates Announced," ibid., February 27, 1942, p. 29; "Vote Set July 23 on Stock Fee Rise," ibid., July 11, 1953, p. 19; "NYSE Governors Back Average 13% Rise," ibid., March 21, 1958, p. 1; New York Stock Exchange, *Factbook* (New York: NYSE, 1972), p. 60.

Notes

Notes

Chapter 1
The Brokerage Industry

1. This estimate has appeared in a number of advertisements including, "Financial Freedom. How Merrill, Lynch could help you get and keep it.", *Wall Street Journal*, May 14, 1974, p. 21.

2. In its voluminous *Report of the Special Study of the Securities Markets of the SEC*, hereafter called the *Special Study*, the SEC cites examples of brokers who were unable to read basic financial statements. The Commission found the majority of registered representatives to be uninformed with respect to the executing, cashiering, and clearing functions notwithstanding the fact that all but ten percent of applicants pass the New York Stock Exchange examinations in those topics (*Special Study*, Part 1, pp. 109-112).

3. The broker's share varies with the gross revenue he produces and the types of securites sold. Larger producers usually receive a greater portion of the commissions they generate. The salesman's share is also greater on specialty items like municipal bonds and new issues, which are more profitable for the brokerage house.

4. It is typical, for example, for a broker who changes firms to retain most of his accounts.

5. In 1972, 52,635 stock brokers and 100,365 back office personnel were employed by member firms of the New York Stock Exchange according to its *1972 Factbook*, p. 81.

6. Instead, certificates may be processed through a stock clearing corporation operated by the exchange. By pairing up complementary executed transactions between different brokerage houses, those organizations make it unnecessary to clear each transaction separately. Approximately thirty percent of NYSE transactions are processed through the Exchange Clearing Corportion. G.L. Leffler and L.C. Farwell, *The Stock Market*, p. 285.

7. Bache and Co., "Some very important members of your investing team you may never meet," advertisement, *Forbes*, May 1, 1974, p. 37.

8. Donald T. Regan, *A View from the Street*, p. 95.

9. *Special Study*, Part 1, p. 146.

10. See, for example, the SEC *1969 Annual Report*, p. 1; or Hurd Baruch, *Wall Street: Security Risk*, p. 105.

11. Source: NYSE, op. cit., p. 64. Included in the cost of offices is boardroom equipment and branch office communications.

12. This was discussed, for example, in "Brokerage Houses which are Managing to Earn Profits during the Bull Market," *New York Times*, June 14, 1970, Section 3, p. 1.

13. NYSE, op. cit., p. 65.

14. J.W. Hazard and M. Christie, *The Investment Business*, p. 104.

15. Frederick Amling, *Investments*, p. 226.

16. SEC, *1972 Annual Report*, p. 163.

17. Most mutual funds retailed by brokerage houses charge an initial 8.5 percent commission. Because this is subtracted from the amount of the purchase, the commission is 8.5/91.5 = 9.3% of the amount actually invested. Irwin Friend, et al., *Mutual Funds and Other Institutional Investors*, p. 52.

18. NYSE, op. cit., p. 64.

19. While sales figures are unavailable, only 4587 of 53,000 registered representatives were authorized to sell insurance. Even fewer deal in real estate and tax shelters. Frederick Andrews, "Securities Firms Seek to Diversify to Offset Stock Market's Cycles," *Wall Street Journal*, December 12, 1972, p. 1.

20. NYSE, loc. cit.

21. In support of this view, the president of A.G. Edwards has told shareholders, "Our willingness to diversify into other areas than stock brokerage is limited to those activities which would be supportive to the successful operation of our branches." (*1972 Annual Report*, p. 2.)

Chapter 2
Organization of the Industry

1. W.J. Eiteman, et al., *The Stock Market*, p. 51.

2. From eighty to ninety percent of regional trading was estimated to involve NYSE listed stocks by James E. Walter in *The Role of the Regional Securities Exchanges*, p. 30.

3. Figures are taken from the prospectuses of the common stock offerings of publicly owned NYSE member firms: Merrill, Lynch, Pierce, Fenner, and Smith, p. 15; Bache and Co., p. 25; E.F. Hutton and Co., p. 15; Dean Witter and Co., p. 23; Paine, Webber, Jackson and Curtis, p. 43; Reynolds Securities, p. 15; CBWL-Hayden, Stone,

p. 21; Mitchum, Jones, and Templeton, p. 18; A.G. Edwards and Sons, p. 14; Piper, Jaffray and Hopwood, p. 10; Jas. H. Oliphant and Co., p. 13; First of Michigan Corp., p. 16.

4. F. Amling, *Investments*, p. 233.

5. SEC, *1972 Annual Report*, p. 158. See Table 3-1.

6. *Special Study*, Part 2, p. 844. Characteristics of the Third and Fourth Markets are assessed in detail by Sydney Robbins, *The Securities Markets: Operations and Issues*, pp. 252-261.

7. Comparable regulation and disclosure requirements were not extended to the over the counter market until adoption of the Securities Act of 1964.

8. Richard R. West and Seha M. Tinic, *The Economics of the Stock Market*, p. 228.

9. SEC, *1972 Annual Report*, p. 157.

10. Only one firm has isolated NYSE revenue. Over the five year period 1967-1971, Exchange commissions accounted for an average of 62.9 percent of the gross brokerage income of Jas. H. Oliphant and Co., Inc. Oliphant is a small brokerage house transacting less than one-quarter of one percent of NYSE business. Oliphant, *Prospectus*, p. 13.

11. J.W. Hazard and M. Christie, *The Investment Business*, p. 153.

12. Robbins, op. cit., p. 202.

13. George J. Stigler, "Price and Nonprice Competition," *Journal of Political Economy*, vol. 72, February 1968, p. 149. Barriers to entry are described as "stringent" by West and Tinic, op. cit., p. 111.

14. H.G. Manne, ed., *Economic Policy and the Regulation of Corporate Securities*, p. 228.

15. Since February, 1973, the Exchange has permitted broker-dealer affiliates of mutual funds and other institutional investors to be members only if they do at least eighty percent of their securities business with the public. While favored by NYSE members, this rule was prompted by the SEC; "SEC Adopts Rule for Institution's Exchange Seats," *Wall Street Journal*, February 15, 1973, p. 3.

16. Manne, loc. cit.

17. Figures are taken from Peter Wycoff, *Wall Street and the Stock Markets*, pp. 150, 151. A regular market is made in Exchange seats. Persons wishing to trade seats so inform the Exchange secretary who publishes the highest bid and lowest asked price.

18. Because each member was given the right to one-quarter share in an additional seat in February 1929, pre-1929 figures were reduced by twenty percent.

19. "Three Seats on Big Board Are Sold for $85,000," *Wall Street Journal*, May 15, 1974, p. 25.

20. This follows from the principle that any (expected) flow of income can be expressed as a stock, a theme which motivates the theories of interest associated with Fisher, Knight, and Friedman. It appears to be well recognized that seat prices capitalize industry profits. See Alfred E. Kahn, *The Economics of Regulation*, vol. 2, p. 209.

21. Robert Sobel, *The Big Board: A History of the New York Stock Exchange*, chapter 12.

22. D.T. Regan, *A View from the Street*, pp. 92, 93.

23. *The Monopoly Power of the NYSE*, pp. 47-85. Doede's work was supervised by three economists who have made extensive contributions to the literature of nonprice competition and the brokerage industry: George J. Stigler, Harold Demsetz, and Lester Telser.

24. Amling, op. cit., p. 47.

25. NYSE, *1972 Factbook*, p. 81, and SEC, *1972 Annual Report*, p. 146.

26. NYSE, "Economic Effects of Negotiated Commission Rates on the Brokerage Industry," a report submitted to the SEC in August, 1968 (hereafter called "Economic Effects"). The figures are quoted in West and Tinic, op. cit., pp. 130 and 133.

27. U.S. Senate, Committee on the Judiciary, Subcommittee on Antitrust and Monopoly, *Concentration Ratios in Manufacturing Industries: 1963*, Part 1. The median ratio was 55 percent.

Chapter 3
Noncompetitive Pricing

1. Quoted in E.C. Stedman, ed., *The New York Stock Exchange*, pp. 502, 503.

2. F. Amling, *Investments*, p. 282.

3. With other "member firms that have a long record for going out and attracting new business," Merrill, Lynch resisted both the 1954 and 1958 rises; "Wall Street Is Split on Raising Fees," *New York Times*, March 22, 1958, p. 23.

4. In a December 2, 1970 speech, the president of Merrill, Lynch stated his firm's argument as follows: "We say that competition is good for everyone. We base our investment advice on the competitive

stance of the company we are analyzing. The price of a stock is set by forces operative in the marketplace. Yet we live with this anomaly of a fixed rate structure. We live as exceptions to our own rules." Quoted in H. Baruch, *Wall Street: Security Risk*, p. 291.

5. J.W. Hazard and M. Christie, *The Investment Business*, p. 373.

6. Firms controlling one third of the Exchange seats account for only three percent of NYSE commissions (ibid., p. 373). The scale economies of large firms are demonstrated by statistical analysis presented in the NYSE "Economic Effects" brief, submitted to the SEC in August 1968. The Chairman of the SEC agrees with this result according to R. Rustin and K. Bacon in "Regional Brokers Say End of Fixed Rates Won't Bring Collapse," *Wall Street Journal*, May 29, 1974, p. 1. R.R. West and S.M. Tinic, *The Economics of the Stock Market*, also discuss such cost differences (pp. 108-139).

7. "Move to Increase Stock Trade Rates," *New York Times*, May 8, 1919, p. 24.

8. "Schedule of Rates Proposed by Governors of NYSE," *New York Times*, October 27, 1924, p. 35.

9. "Exchange to Vote on Fee Increases," *New York Times*, December 16, 1937, p. 43.

10. S. Robbins, *The Securities Markets*, p. 177.

11. The sales, execution, clearing, and cashiering costs associated with orders of various size differ in proportion to the value of the trade. To reflect properly these differences, the commission schedule's sliding scale should be based on an analysis of the cost of components of brokerage service. Robbins, op. cit., pp. 178-180 offers a detailed discussion of the theory of rate structure.

12. Stedman, loc. cit.

13. Disorderly conduct carries a fine of $50.00. Exchange members who do not honor their stated bid and asked prices can be assessed a $20.00 penalty; ibid., pp. 497, 498, and 504. Even the relatively serious infraction of not meeting the Exchange net capital rule does not lead to suspension; "Big Board Unit Fines Stern, Doubuler $2500 On Net Capital Rule," *Wall Street Journal*, May 17, 1974, p. 21.

14. Stedman, op. cit., pp. 502, 503.

15. Sobel, op. cit., pp. 237, 238.

16. Source Securities Corporation, *Saving Money on Commissions* (p. 3); Daley, Coolidge, and Co., *Reduce Your Securities Commissions* (p. 3). Savings of up to fifty-six percent are quoted by Charles

Schwab and Co., "New! Reduced Brokerage Commissions," advertisement, *Wall Street Journal*, June 20, 1974, p. 27. Due to the comparatively small size of most third market houses, cost savings might be even greater were NYSE firms to compete with respect to price.

17. Richard Martin, "Many Investors Turn to Firms that Discount their Fees on Stocks," *Wall Street Journal*, January 9, 1973, p. 1.

18. Since 1965, the SEC has maintained the data set "Over the Counter Dollar Volume in Common Stocks Listed on the New York Stock Exchange." These data were provided by the Commission's Office of Over the Counter Regulation.

19. Merrill, Lynch, *Prospectus*, p. 19; Bache and Co., *Prospectus*, pp. 13 and 24.

20. At least some broker costs (e.g. those associated with data transmission and the clearing function) would not rise with the price of the securities involved in a transaction.

21. The average price on round lot trades was between $40.00 and $50.00 (1968 dollars) during the 1960s; NYSE, *1972 Factbook*, p. 71.

22. The Bureau of Labor Statistics' wholesale price indices reproduced in the U.S. Bureau of the Census, *Historical Statistics of the U.S. 1960*, pp. 116, 117 and the *Economic Report of the President, 1972*, p. 250 were spliced and expressed in 1968 dollars. The Standard and Poors 500 common stock index, available in the latter source, was also deflated to 1968 levels. Calculations were made using a computer program written by the author.

Chapter 4
Regulation

1. Historian Ralph F. DeBedts links the formation of the SEC with the personal attitudes towards speculation of Roosevelt and his "Brain Trust," Moley, Berle, and Tugwell; *The New Deal's SEC: The Formative Years*, pp. 30-34.

2. The SEC has been responsible for very little analysis of the welfare and efficiency implications of competitive practices within the industry. The staff and members of the Commission are primarily lawyers. For this reason, regulation has centered upon application of the seven acts of Congress for which the SEC is responsible without

regard to competitive concerns; S. Robbins, *The Security Markets*, pp. 79-80.

3. This position was stated during a SEC hearing, "In the matter of Richard Witney," quoted in the *Special Study*, Part 4, p. 308. While SEC Chairman, William O. Douglas expressed similar sentiments according to DeBedts, op. cit., p. 15.

4. *Special Study*, Part 4, p. 698.

5. Section 19(b)9, 15 U.S. Code 78, S(6) quoted by A.E. Kahn, in *The Economics of Regulation*, vol. 2, p. 194.

6. Part 1, p. 111.

7. Lee Silberman, "Critical Examination of SEC Proposals," *Harvard Business Review*, November 1964, p. 121.

8. Kahn, op. cit., p. 195.

9. Robbins, op. cit., p. 295.

10. *1967 Annual Report*, p. 56.

11. Kahn, loc. cit.

12. In a letter to the Senate Committee on Banking and Currency, the Commission Chairman went so far as to request clarifying legislation granting Exchange members "antitrust immunity in areas subject to (SEC) review." Such legislation was not forthcoming. *Congressional Record–Senate*, 89th Congress, First Session, August 2, 1965, p. 18312.

13. Robbins, op. cit., pp. 70, 121, 177.

14. Quoted in H.G. Manne, ed., *Economic Policy and the Regulation of Corporate Securities*, p. 333.

15. Robbins, op. cit., p. 118.

16. The implications of such a policy are discussed in Chapter 8.

17. Robbins, op. cit., pp. 176, 177.

18. Loc. cit.

19. SEC, *1972 Annual Report*, p. 8.

20. J.W. Hazard and M. Christie, *The Investment Business*, p. 368.

21. D.T. Regan, *A View from the Street*, p. 117n.

22. Kahn, op. cit., p. 197. The SEC objected to the practice by mutual funds of using give-ups to recompense brokers who had sold their shares. By increasing the assets they controlled, mutual fund managers were using commissions paid by fund owners for self gain in the official view.

23. Reacting to Congressional support for unrestricted entry by institutions, the Commission "expressed its intention to exercise appropriate authority to ensure that the exchanges adopt rules

requiring that members must conduct a predominant portion of their brokerage commission business with and for nonaffiliated public customers," *1972 Annual Report*, p. 8. On February 15, 1973 the SEC directed the NYSE to forbid membership to firms which did less than eighty percent of their business with the public.

24. *Special Study*, Part 1, p. 79.

25. The SEC's record in its other area of responsibility, regulation of the securities markets, appears to be little better. In evaluating the effect of SEC supervision related to investor protection, George Stigler discovered no significant difference between pre-SEC and post-SEC public stock offerings. In both periods, investors could expect to lose about one-third of their new issue investment within one year of purchase. "Public Regulation of the Securities Markets' Operations," *Journal of Business*, vol. 37, April 1964, p. 121.

Chapter 5
Nonprice Competition

1. Merrill, Lynch, Pierce, Fenner and Smith, *Prospectus*, p. 25.

2. In its *1972 Annual Report*, Paine, Webber, Jackson, and Curtis describes the "Compuscan" system, which monitors statistics on 1500 stocks. That system is similar to Dean Witter's somewhat larger "Compare" facility (Dean Witter and Co., *1972 Annual Report*, p. 18). William O'Neil and Co., a pioneer in computer securities analysis, has developed a sophisticated on-line capability which handles some 200 million pieces of information ("If knowing when to get in takes genius, . . . ," advertisement, *Business Week*, May 11, 1974, p. 11).

3. Technical analysis is directed toward the trading characteristics of a stock including its price and volume patterns. Fundamental analysis, in contrast, is based on the firm's earnings, operations, and future prospects as a productive entity.

4. Walston and Co. estimated that it prints 437,000 copies of its market letter daily. *Special Study*, Part 1, p. 330.

5. Such firms as Spencer, Trask; Baker, Weeks; and Smith, Barney are referred to as research-oriented houses in the financial press. This method of differentiation is illustrated by a comparison of two firms cited in the *Special Study*, Part 1, p. 351: in 1963 Bruns, Nordeman and Co. employed one part-time research analyst

to advise customers of its 74 brokers; Smith, Barney, in contrast, maintained a research staff of 26 analysts for 113 registered representatives.

6. Paine, Webber, Jackson, and Curtis, *1972 Annual Report*, p. 6.

7. See, for example, A.G. Edwards and Sons, *Who We Are . . . How We Work For You* (p. 26). Many firms maintain offices in vacation centers in the U.S. and abroad.

8. Paine, Webber, Jackson, and Curtis, *1972 Annual Report*, p. 46.

9. Dean Witter and Co., *1972 Annual Report*, p. 1.

10. Donaldson, Lufkin, and Jenrette, Inc., *1971 Annual Report*, p. 11.

11. Dean Witter and Co., *1972 Annual Report*, p. 12.

12. One institutionally oriented firm, Donaldson, Lufkin, and Jenrette, Inc., described its corporate strategy: "Accelerating change has marked the past decade (in the securities industry) and DLJ has moved to meet the challenge . . . through our basic strengths in institutional services." (Op. cit., p. 1.)

13. Dean Witter and Co., introduced a plan under which $25,000 of commercial paper could be purchased for a brokerage fee of $6.25. Banks and firms which have traditionally been in this market charge from $20.00 to $25.00 for the same service. Dean Witter does not act as a principal in such transactions so it receives no indirect remuneration.

14. Dean Witter and Co., *1972 Annual Report*, p. 12.

15. Richard E. Rustin, "Hayden, Stone, Shearson Discuss Possible Merger," *Wall Street Journal*, May 29, 1974, p. 3. One reason for a proposed merger between a firm providing this service and one which doesn't is to extend coverage to the customers of the uninsured firm (ibid.).

16. "NASD to Offer Firms Additional Insurance on Client's Accounts," *Wall Street Journal*, May 14, 1974, p. 10.

17. The practice of using advisory services to make contact with customers is documented by J.W. Hazard and M. Christie, *The Investment Business*, p. 56.

18. For example, full page advertisements in national magazines publicized new services of William O'Neil and Co. (O'Neil, op. cit.); and Kuhn, Loeb and Co. ("We are pleased to announce the opening of a West Coast office," *Business Week*, March 30, 1974, p. 86C-W). In the same way, Josephthal and Co., announced "Of course your

account with us is insured," advertisement, *Wall Street Journal*, March 15, 1974, p. 15.

19. "Brokerage Houses which Are Managing to Earn Profits during the Bull Market," *New York Times*, June 14, 1970, Section 3, p. 1.

20. "Merrill Making its Move for Street's Top Analysts," *Wall Street Letter*, vol. 6, April 8, 1974, p. 1.

21. Dean Witter and Co., *1972 Annual Report*, p. 16.

22. Dana L. Thomas, "Analysts' Insecurity," *Barron's*, May 27, 1974, p. 3.

23. *Wall Street Letter*, op. cit., p. 1.

24. Merrill, Lynch, *Prospectus*, p. 17.

25. R.E. Rustin and K. Bacon, "Regional Brokers Say End of Fixed Rates Won't Bring Collapse," *Wall Street Journal*, May 29, 1974, p. 1.

26. L. Silberman, "Critical Examination of SEC Proposals," *Harvard Business Review*, November 1964, p. 128; Robbins, *The Securities Markets*, p. 184. In addition, each of the twelve prospectuses cited in Chapter 1 refers to these aspects of the industry as "intensively competitive." See, for example, Merrill, Lynch, p. 32; Dean Witter, pp. 4, 32; and First of Michigan, p. 29.

27. *Special Study* cited in Hazard and Christie, op. cit., p. 214.

28. NYSE, *Factbook*, 1966-1973. Included in the cost of offices is boardroom equipment and branch office communications.

29. "Brokerage Houses which Are Managing to Earn Profits during the Bull Market," *New York Times*, June 14, 1970, Section 3, p. 1.

30. R. Martin, "Many Investors Turn to Firms that Discount their Fees on Stocks," *Wall Street Journal*, January 9, 1973, p. 1.

31. Frederic M. Scherer, *Industrial Market Structure and Economic Performance*, p. 336. L.G. Telser, "Advertising and Cigarettes," *Journal of Political Economy*, vol. 70, 1962, pp. 471-499.

32. Scherer, loc. cit.

33. Hazard and Christie, op. cit., p. 56.

34. Ibid., p. 226; Robbins, loc. cit.

35. Merrill, Lynch offers a discount of from sixteen to twenty-five percent in its pioneer program (*Sharebuilder Plan*, p. 1). The Paine, Webber "Econo-Trade" program reduces fees by fifteen percent. Bache and Co. promises twenty-five percent savings in "Term-Trade" accounts (*Term-Trade*, p. 3). Restrictions vary between the plans. However, they typically do not include stock transfer services. Customers must also place orders and pay for stock one day prior to the transaction. Merrill, Lynch asks customers to mail in their orders.

36. In the week after introducing its Sharebuilder plan, Merrill, Lynch received two and one-half times the normal number of new accounts. However, Paine, Webber was less successful. Both firms acknowledge that it will be some time before a valid assessment of the plans can be made. "Cut-rate Plans for Stock Purchases," *Wall Street Journal*, April 11, 1974, p. 1.

37. For example, Merrill, Lynch offers discounts on transactions involving less than $2,000 only. The Bache plan covers stock positions held for 35 days or less.

Chapter 6
The Theory of Nonprice Competition with Price Collusion

1. Alfred Marshall, *Principles of Economics* (New York: Macmillan Publishing Co., 1920), p. 458, and Irving Fisher, *Elementary Principles of Economics* (New York: Macmillan Publishing Co., 1913), p. 323.

2. *Studies in Economics of Overhead Costs* (Chicago: The University of Chicago Press, 1923), p. 418.

3. "Cost of Production and Price over Long and Short Periods," *Journal of Political Economy*, vol. 29, 1921, p. 332.

4. "The Laws of Returns Under Competitive Conditions," *Economic Journal*, vol. 36, 1926, pp. 535-550.

5. Chamberlin, op. cit., p. 5.

6. Ibid., p. 60.

7. For example, E.S. Rogers concludes that there "is no element of monopoly involved at all in . . . trademark(s)" in *Goodwill, Trademarks, and Unfair Trading* (Chicago: A.W. Shaw, 1914), p. 14.

8. In Richard Ely, *Outlines of Economics*, 5th ed., pp. 562-563, quoted by Chamberlin, op. cit., p. 302.

9. Chamberlin, op. cit., p. 56.

10. "Imperfect Competition Revisited," *Economic Journal*, September 1953, p. 579.

11. Chamberlin, op. cit.; "Product Heterogeneity and Public Policy Welfare Economics," *American Economic Review*, May 1950; "Monopolistic Competition Revisited," *Economica*, November 1951; "Some Aspects of Nonprice Competition" in *The Role and Nature of Competition in Our Marketing Economy*, Harvey W. Huegy, ed.,

University of Illinois Bulletin, vol. 51, no. 76, June 1954; *Monopoly and Competition and Their Regulation. Papers and Proceedings of a Conference Held by the International Economic Association*, London, 1954; *Towards a More General Theory of Value*; and " 'Full Cost' and Monopolistic Competition," *Economic Journal*, vol. 72, June 1962. Chamberlin seems to have been obsessed with this theme of personal product differentiation.

12. Robert Triffin, *Monopolistic Competition and General Equilibrium Theory*, pp. 47 and 57.

13. Joan Robinson, *The Economics of Imperfect Competition*, pp. 89-90.

14. Chamberlin, *The Theory of Monopolistic Competition*, pp. 8 and 56.

15. R.J. Hall and C.J. Hitch, "Price Theory and Business Behavior," *Oxford Economic Papers*, No. 2, May 1939, p. 15; Paul M. Sweezy, "Demand Under Conditions of Oligopoly," *Journal of Political Economy*, vol. 47, August 1939, pp. 568-573; and J.M. Clark, "Towards a Concept of Workable Competition," *American Economic Review*, vol. 30, June 1940, pp. 241-256.

16. See, for example, the work of Harold Demsetz: "The Welfare and Empirical Implications of Monopolistic Competition," *Economic Journal*, vol. 74, September 1964; "Do Competition and Monopolistic Competition Differ?" *Journal of Political Economy*, vol. 77, January/February 1969, pp. 21-30.

17. Triffin, op. cit., pp. 78-95 and R.L. Bishop, "Elasticities, Cross-Elasticities, and Market Relationships," *American Economic Review*, vol. 42, December 1952, pp. 779-803.

18. Federal Reserve System research has provided an extensive literature on banking markets. Over forty marketing books printed between 1933 and 1954 cited Chamberlin's theory according to E.T. Grether's article in Robert E. Kuenne, ed., *Monopolistic Competition Theory: Studies In Impact*, chapter 15. An early application of the theory to agricultural economics was due to George Stigler, "A Generalization of the Theory of Imperfect Competition," *Journal of Farm Economics*, 1937.

19. W.J. Baumol, "On the Theory of Expansion of the Firm," *American Economic Review*, vol. 52, December 1962, pp. 1078-1087; O.E. Williamson, "Managerial Discretion and Business Behavior," *American Economic Review*, vol. 53, December 1963, pp. 1032-1057; Ira Horowitz, *Decision Making and the Theory of the Firm*, pp. 409-411.

20. R.W. Jostram, "A Treatment of Distributed Lags in the Theory of Advertising Expenditures," *Journal of Marketing*, vol. 20, 1955, pp. 36-46; and Richard B. Heflebower in Kuenne, op. cit., chapter 8.

21. W.S. Comanor and T.A. Wilson, "Market Structure, Advertising, and Market Performance: An Empirical Analysis," *Review of Economics and Statistics*, vol. 49, November 1967, pp. 423-440; William G. Shepherd, "The Elements of Market Structure," *Review of Economics and Statistics*, vol. 54, February 1972, pp. 25-37; and L.G. Telser, "Advertising and Competition," *Journal of Political Economy*, vol. 72, 1964, pp. 541-546.

22. B. Imel and P. Helmberger, "Estimation of Structure-Profit Relationships with Application to the Food Processing Sector," *American Economic Review*, vol. 61, September 1971, pp. 614-627; and L.G. Telser, "Advertising and Cigarettes," *Journal of Political Economy*, vol. 52, October 1962, pp. 471-499.

23. Alfred E. Kahn considers airline rivalry through customer service (*The Economics of Regulation*, vol. 2, pp. 209-216). William A. Jordan examines improvements in the quality of passenger travel through the introduction of new aircraft in *Airline Regulation in America* (Baltimore: Johns-Hopkins Press, 1970). Regulation of service competition is analyzed by Stanley C. Hollander, *Passenger Transportation, Readings from a Marketing Point of View* (East Lansing: Michigan State University, 1968), pp. 580-589.

24. See pp. 42, 43 in Chapter 5.

25. The result that the inability of firms to collude with respect to a variable leads to pervasive competition is not alien to economic theory: Marshallian analysis tells us that in industries where, due to market size or antitrust regulation, price cannot be collusively established, price cutters will force price to average cost. This occurs even where competitors have the sophistication to realize that their action will eliminate profit.

26. George J. Stigler, *The Organization of Industry*, pp. 23-26; Horowitz, op. cit., pp. 167-171.

27. Chamberlin, *The Theory of Monopolistic Competition*, chapter 6.

28. The most rigorous treatment of this classic problem is Stigler's "A Theory of Oligopoly," *Journal of Political Economy*, vol. 72, February 1964.

29. *D* may shift out somewhat if increased customer services attract new customers to the industry. Demand from existing customers will remain unchanged, however.

30. This thesis is consistent with Gardiner Means's concept of competitive sales promotion. Means found that with price coordination and limited entry, nonprice competition absorbs the economic profit of steel producers: "In some situations it could be expected that prices would be in the nature of monopoly prices and monopoly profits would be eliminated by a wasteful rise in costs." *Pricing Power and the Public Interest*, p. 214.

Chapter 7
The Empirical Evidence

1. This has the obvious disadvantage that brokerage personnel and facilities differ in cost and productivity. However, measuring customer service output by factor employment rather than cost eliminates the need to account for changing factor prices.

2. Chapter 9 of Henri Theil, *Principles of Econometrics*, contains an outstanding introduction to simultaneous systems including two-stage estimation procedures (pp. 429-483).

3. The technique estimates a polynomial expression which approximates the lag structure giving the best fit. J. Johnston, *Econometric Methods*, 2nd ed., offers a particularly lucid explanation of the process (pp. 292-300).

4. Theil, op. cit., pp. 460-461.

5. D. Cochrane and G.H. Orcutt, "Application of Least Squares Regression to Relationships Containing Autocorrelated Error Terms," *Journal of the American Statistical Association*, 1949, pp. 32-61. For a more intuitive exposition see J.L. Murphy, *Introductory Econometrics*, pp. 314-322.

6. Data were acquired from several sources. NYSE and regional exchange dollar volume figures are from the SEC *1972 Annual Report*, p. 157. Peter Wycoff's *Wall Street and the Stock Markets* contains historical NYSE seat prices and stock volume. Commission rates were calculated from the schedules printed in *New York Times* articles cited in chapter 3. Figures for N_b, N_e and N_o were taken from the NYSE *Factbook* (1956-1972) and its predecessor, the *Yearbook* (1939-1955).

7. Estimations were made using the *Econometric Software Package*, a computer program, (Cambridge: Massachusetts Institute of Technology, December 1972). Equations 2 and 4b are based on the

sample period 1950-1972 while the other relationships were estimated using data from 1942 to 1972.

8. The coefficient on V in equation 1 is significantly different from zero at the 90% level; T in equations 1 and 2 and C in equation 4b are significant at the 92.5% level; C in equation 4a and the nonprice competition variables in 4b and 4c are significant at the 95% level; all other coefficients hold at the 99.5% level.

9. This is consistent with Walter Oi's hypothesis that certain types of labor are quasi-fixed factors of production; "Labor as a Quasi-fixed Factor," *Journal of Political Economy*, vol. 70, December 1962, pp. 538-555.

10. The calculations were made in a double precision FORTRAN program written by the author.

Bibliography

Bibliography

Books

Amling, Frederick. *Investments.* N.J.: Prentice-Hall, 1970.

Baruch, Hurd. *Wall Street: Security Risk.* Baltimore: Penguin Books, 1972.

Baumol, William J. *The Stock Market and Economic Efficiency.* New York: Fordham, 1965.

Chamberlin, Edward H. *The Theory of Monopolistic Competition.* Cambridge: Harvard University Press, 1933.

_______. *Towards a More General Theory of Value.* New York: Oxford University Press, 1957.

Doede, Robert. *The Monopoly Power of the New York Stock Exchange*, unpublished dissertation, University of Chicago, June 1967.

Dougall, Herbert E. *Investments.* 9th ed. Englewood Cliffs, N.J.: Prentice-Hall, 1973.

Eiteman, W.J., et al. *The Stock Market.* 4th ed. New York: McGraw-Hill Book Company, 1966.

Fergeson, C.E. *Microeconomic Theory.* Homewood, Ill.: Richard D. Irwin, 1969.

Friend, Irwin, et al. *The Over the Counter Securities Markets.* New York: McGraw-Hill Book Company, 1958.

_______. *Mutual Funds and Other Institutional Investors.* New York: McGraw-Hill Book Company, 1970.

Hazard, J.W. and Christie, M. *The Investment Business.* New York: Harper and Row Publishers, 1964.

Horowitz, Ira. *Decision Making and the Theory of the Firm.* New York: Holt, Rinehart and Winston, 1970.

Jordan, William A. *Airline Regulation in America.* Baltimore: Johns Hopkins Press, 1970.

Kahn, Alfred E. *The Economics of Regulation.* vol. 2. New York: John Wiley and Sons, 1971.

Kuenne, Robert E., ed. *Monopolistic Competition Theory: Studies in Impact.* New York: John Wiley and Sons, 1967.

Leffler, G.L. and Farwell, L.C. *The Stock Market.* 3rd ed. New York: Ronald, 1963.

Manne, H.G., ed. *Economic Policy and the Regulation of Corporate*

Securities. Washington, D.C.: American Enterprise Institute for Public Policy Research, 1969.

Means, Gardner C. *Pricing Power and the Public Interest*. New York: Harper, 1962.

National Association of Securities Dealers, *Manual*. Washington: NASD, 1967.

New York Stock Exchange (Committee on Public Relations). *Fact-book*. New York: NYSE, 1956-1973.

______ . *Yearbook*. New York: NYSE, 1939-1955.

Regan, Donald T. *A View from the Street*. New York: New American Library, 1972.

Robbins, Sydney. *The Securities Markets: Operations and Issues*. New York: Free Press, 1966.

Robinson, Joan. *The Economics of Imperfect Competition*. 2nd ed. London: Macmillan & Co., 1969.

Scherer, Frederick M. *Industrial Market Structure and Economic Performance*. Chicago: Rand McNally and Co., 1971.

Stigler, George J. *The Organization of Industry*. Homewood, Ill.: Richard D. Irwin, 1968.

Triffin, Robert. *Monopolistic Competition and General Equilibrium Theory*. Cambridge: Harvard University Press, 1962.

Walter, James E. *The Role of the Regional Securities Exchanges*. Berkeley: University of California Press, 1957.

West, Richard R., and Tinic, Seha M. *The Economics of the Stock Market*. New York: Praeger, 1971.

Broker Publications

Bache and Co. *Prospectus*. New York: September 16, 1971.

______ . "Some very important members of your investing team you may never meet," advertisement, *Forbes*, May 1, 1974, p. 37.

______ . *Term-Trade*. New York: 1974.

CBWL-Hayden, Stone. *Prospectus*. New York: October 1, 1971.

Charles Schwab and Co. "New! Reduced Brokerage Commissions," advertisement, *Wall Street Journal*, June 20, 1974, p. 27.

Daley, Coolidge, and Co. *Reduce Your Securities Commissions*. New York: 1974.

Dean Witter and Co. *1972 Annual Report*. San Francisco: 1972.

______ . *Prospectus*. San Francisco: February 9, 1972.

Donaldson, Lufkin, and Jenrette, Inc. *1972 Annual Report.* New York: 1972.
_______ . *Prospectus.* New York: April 9, 1970.
A.G. Edwards and Sons. *1972 Annual Report.* St. Louis: 1972.
_______ . *Who We Are . . . How We Work For You.* St. Louis: 1974.
_______ . *Prospectus.* St. Louis: November 17, 1971.
First Boston Corp. *Prospectus.* New York: May 3, 1972.
First of Michigan Corp. *Prospectus.* Detroit: June 14, 1972.
E.F. Hutton and Co. *Prospectus.* New York: April 25, 1972.
Merrill, Lynch, Pierce, Fenner, and Smith. "Financial Freedom. How Merrill Lynch could help you get it and keep it," advertisement, *Wall Street Journal*, May 14, 1974, p. 21.
_______ . *Prospectus.* New York: September 13, 1972.
_______ . *Sharebuilder Plan.* New York: 1974.
Mitchum, Jones, and Templeton. *Prospectus.* Los Angeles: March 21, 1972.
Jas. H. Oliphant and Co. *Prospectus.* New York: June 14, 1972.
William O'Neil and Co., "If knowing when to get in takes genius . . . ," advertisement, *Business Week*, May 11, 1974, p. 11.
Paine, Webber, Jackson and Curtis. *1972 Annual Report.* New York: 1972.
_______ . *Prospectus.* New York: March 9, 1972.
Piper, Jaffray and Hopwood. *Prospectus.* Minneapolis: July 29, 1971.
Reynolds Securities. *Prospectus.* New York: November 9, 1971.
Source Securities Corp. *Saving Money on Commissions.* New York: 1974.
Weeden and Co. *Prospectus.* New York: June 17, 1971.

Government Publications

U.S. Bureau of the Census. *Historical Statistics of the United States.* Washington: Government Printing Office, 1960.
U.S. Department of Commerce. *Business Statistics.* Washington: Government Printing Office, 1971.
_______ . *Survey of Current Business.* Washington: Government Printing Office, 1971-1973.
U.S. Securities and Exchange Commission. *Annual Report.* Washington: Government Printing Office, 1967-1973.
_______ . *Report of the Special Study of the Securities Markets of the SEC.* House Document 95. 88th Congress, 1st Session, 1963.

U.S. Securities and Exchange Commission, U.S. Senate, Committee on the Judiciary, Subcommittee on Antitrust and Monopoly. *Concentration Ratios in Manufacturing Industries: 1963.* Washington: Government Printing Office, 1966.

Histories

DeBedts, Ralph F. *The New Deal's SEC: The Formative Years.* New York: Columbia University Press, 1964.

Sobel, Robert. *The Big Board: A History of the New York Stock Exchange.* New York: Free Press, 1965.

Stedman, E.C., ed. *The New York Stock Exchange.* vol. 1. New York: Greenwood, 1905.

Wyckoff, Peter. *Wall Street and the Stock Markets.* Philadelphia: Chilton, 1972.

Periodicals

Andrews, Frederick, "Securities Firms Seek to Diversify to Offset Stock Market's Cycles," *Wall Street Journal*, December 12, 1972, pp. 1, 2.

Baxter, W.F., "NYSE Commission Rates: A Private Cartel Goes Public," *Stanford Law Review*, vol. 22, April 1970, pp. 672-712.

"Big Board Unit Fines Stern, Doubuler $2500 on Net Capital Rule," *Wall Street Journal*, May 17, 1974, p. 21.

"Brokerage Houses which Are Managing to Earn Profits during the Bull Market," *New York Times*, June 14, 1970, Section 3, p. 1.

Chamberlin, Edward H., "Monopolistic Competition Revisited," *Economica*, November 1951, pp. 343-362.

Comanor, W.S. and Wilson, T.A., "Market Structure, Advertising, and Market Performance: An Empirical Analysis," *Review of Economics and Statistics*, vol. 49, November 1967, pp. 423-440.

"Cut-rate Plans for Stock Purchases," *Wall Street Journal*, April 11, 1974, p. 1.

Demsetz, Harold, "Do Competition and Monopolistic Competition Differ?", *Journal of Political Economy*, vol. 76, January/February 1968, pp. 146-148.

"Exchange to Vote on Fee Increases," *New York Times*, December 16, 1937, p. 43.

Martin, Richard, "Many Investors Turn to Firms that Discount their Fees on Stocks," *Wall Street Journal*, January 9, 1973, p. 1.

"Merrill Making its Move for Street's Top Analysts," *Wall Street Letter*, vol. 6, April 8, 1974, p. 1.

"Move to Increase Stock Trade Rates," *New York Times*, May 8, 1919, p. 24.

"NASD to Offer Firms Additional Insurance on Client's Accounts," *Wall Street Journal*, May 14, 1974, p. 10.

"NYSE Governors Back Average 13% Rise," *New York Times*, March 21, 1958, p. 1.

Oi, Walter, "Labor as a Quasi-fixed Factor," *Journal of Political Economy*, vol. 70, December 1962, pp. 538-555.

"Plan to Raise Rates Announced," *New York Times*, February 27, 1942, p. 29.

Rustin, Richard E., "Hayden, Stone, Shearson Discuss Possible Merger," *Wall Street Journal*, May 29, 1974, p. 3.

Rustin, Richard E., and Bacon, Kenneth, "Regional Brokers Say End of Fixed Rates Won't Bring Collapse," ibid., p. 1.

"Schedule of Rates Proposed by Governors Board of NYSE," *New York Times*, October 27, 1924, p. 35.

"SEC Adopts Rule for Institution's Exchange Seats," *Wall Street Journal*, February 15, 1973, p. 3.

Shepherd, William G., "The Elements of Market Structure," *Review of Economics and Statistics*, vol. 54, February 1972, pp. 25-37.

Silberman, Lee, "Critical Examination of SEC Proposals," *Harvard Business Review*, November 1964, pp. 121-132.

Stigler, George J., "Price and Nonprice Competition," *Journal of Political Economy*, vol. 76, February 1968, pp. 149-154.

_______ . "Public Regulation of the Securities Markets' Operations," *Journal of Business*, vol. 37, April 1964, pp. 117-142.

Telser, L.G., "Advertising and Cigarettes," *Journal of Political Economy*, vol. 70, October 1962, pp. 471-499.

_______ . "Advertising and Competition," ibid., vol. 72, 1964, pp. 541-546.

_______ . "Monopolistic Competition: Any Impact Yet:", ibid., vol. 76, March 1968, pp. 312-314.

Thomas, Dana L., "Analysts' Insecurity," *Barron's*, May 27, 1974, p. 3.

"Three Seats on Big Board Are Sold for $85,000," *Wall Street Journal*, May 15, 1974, p. 25.

"Vote Set July 23 on Stock Fee Rise," *New York Times*, July 11, 1953, p. 19.

"Wall Street Is Split on Raising Fees," ibid., March 22, 1958, p. 53.
West, Richard R., and Tinic, Seha M., "Minimum Commission Rates on NYSE Transactions," *Bell Journal of Economics and Management Science*, vol. 2, Autumn 1971, pp. 577-607.

Statistical References

Johnston, J. *Econometric Methods.* 2nd ed. New York: McGraw-Hill Book Company, 1972.
Murphy, James L. *Introductory Econometrics.* Homewood, Ill.: Richard D. Irwin, 1973.
Rebello, Robert E., ed. *Econometric Software Package.* (Computer Program.) Cambridge: Massachusetts Institute of Technology, December 1972 version.
Theil, Henri. *Principles of Econometrics.* New York: John Wiley and Sons, 1971.

Index

Index

About the Author

Lawrence Shepard received the M.A. and Ph.D. degrees in economics from the University of California, Santa Barbara. He was a visiting student at the University of Sussex, England and Christ's College Canterbury in New Zealand. Dr. Shepard's research has included an econometric assessment of the influence of campaign spending on electoral outcome as well as topics related to regulation and the brokerage industry. He has testified in hearings on the impact of California fair trade and drug retailing legislation. Professor Shepard teaches in the Department of Agricultural Economics at the University of California, Davis. He is affiliated with Phi Beta Kappa, the American Economic Association, and the American Association of University Professors.